D0953394

this is the night our house will catch fire

also by nick flynn

this is
the night
our house
will
catch fire

a memoir

nick flynn

W. W. NORTON & COMPANY
Independent Publishers Since 1923

For information about permission to reproduce selections from this book, write to Permissions, W. W. Norton & Company, Inc., 500 Fifth Avenue, New York, NY 10110

For information about special discounts for bulk purchases, please contact W. W. Norton Special Sales at specialsales@wwnorton.com or 800-233-4830

Manufacturing by LSC Communications, Harrisonburg
Book design by Lovedog Studio
Production manager: Beth Steidle

Library of Congress Cataloging-in-Publication Data

Names: Flynn, Nick, 1960– author.
Title: This is the night our house will catch fire : a memoir / Nick Flynn.
Description: First edition. | New York, NY : W. W. Norton & Company, [2020]
Identifiers: LCCN 2019058085 | ISBN 9781324005544 (hardcover) | ISBN 9781324005551 (epub)
Subjects: LCSH: Flynn, Nick, 1960- | Authors, American—21st century—Biography.
Classification: LCC PS3556.L894 Z46 2020 | DDC 818/.603 [B]—dc23
LC record available at https://lccn.loc.gov/2019058085

W. W. Norton & Company, Inc., 500 Fifth Avenue, New York, N.Y. 10110
www.wwnorton.com

W. W. Norton & Company Ltd., 15 Carlisle Street, London W1D 3BS

1 2 3 4 5 6 7 8 9 0

disclaimer: This book began as a story I'd tell my daughter at bedtime, a story about a man who lived in the woods behind my grandmother's house. It was a true story, yet as it unfolded it began to take on the feel of a fairy tale. For this reason, names have been changed in certain instances. Also, in several instances I have taken the liberty of entering into the consciousness of relatives—my mother, my grandfather—and speaking as if I am them. This device is based on shared DNA, memory, letters, and research—not actual transcriptions of their thoughts.

book one

what we first learn about fire
is that we cannot touch it

ice age

FIVE PERFECTLY ROUND STONES, each about the size of
an ostrich egg, sit on my desk in Brooklyn. My daughter
(then seven) had gathered them up from Peggotty Beach on
the last trip we took back to my hometown. The beach is
just off Third Cliff, down from the last house I lived in as
a child. Back then I thought *peggotty* meant "rocky." Now
each stone sits on my desk like an egg in a bird museum, a
diorama showing how all eggs are different—some larger,
some smaller, some speckled, some not. Each is dry now, all
versions of gray. If I touch my tongue anywhere on any one of
them it will come alive.

I was born in the same place as these rocks, in a town formed
by glacier. Ten thousand years ago the sun went away—maybe
it was volcanic ash, maybe a meteorite, maybe God told Noah
to build a boat, told him, *I'm about to kill everyone.* Now
we call it the last ice age. The glacier could push only so far
south, then it stopped—maybe the water was too warm, or
too salty, for it to go on. When the ice receded, all the earth it
had ground into sand was left, and this sand became home to a
native people known as Wampanoag ("People of the Dawn").
Then, after the *Mayflower* came, full of war and disease and
fringy religion, it was christened *Scituate, Massachusetts*—

my hometown. *02066*. From that day on, everyone born in that town has ice in their veins. I was born there, beside the Atlantic, in the shadow of that glacier, and now I don't seem able to escape it. The sound of it. The salt. I need it on my skin. I need to smell it. My mother carried me through the streets of that town inside her. Outside was chaos—lots of drinking, lots of mayhem. Some of this mayhem seeped in, how could it not? When I was born, I came out wrong—two collapsed lungs, staph infection: sickly. For the first two weeks I lived under glass in an incubator, a box like a tiny greenhouse, as if I were a tomato.

Now my job as a father (or one of them) is to tell my daughter stories from when I was her age. Then to bring her back, to show her the source of those stories. So one day she will understand where she is from, what made her. This is the house I lived in when I was your age, this is the saltmarsh I wandered to get to school each day. This is Maria's, where I got my sub the nights my mother was working late. We go to the supermarket and we each buy a donut, hot out of the oil. The enormous mixer my mother used is still there. I'm trying to make it easy for my daughter, something my mother never did for me, though she did a lot. Strange, but I have no idea, still, which house my mother grew up in, and only a vague idea of her hometown, what it was like. Canton is only a few miles from Scituate, maybe half an hour's drive, and even though my mother and I would often drive, especially on the weekend—aimlessly, wandering—we never drove to Canton. She never pointed and said, There, that's the house I grew up in. She rarely, if ever, told me stories of her childhood. It seemed she wanted to get as far away from it as possible, as if we were driving through a dream, or away from a nightmare.

My daughter never met my mother, though she's seen the photos. When she asks how she died I tell her she had a bad heart. This is both a lie and not a lie. When I was having a hard time, I told her it was because I missed my mother, that it was near the anniversary of her death, that I was sad she was gone. This too was both a lie and not a lie. I was thinking of leaving my wife, or, more specifically, I was both thinking and not thinking. This was my chaos. It felt right because I was in control of it. *She would have loved to have met you*, I tell my daughter, which is true, I guess, but how can I know?

The stones on my desk were gathered from the southern edge of Peggotty Beach, where the breakwater meets the sand, where Third Cliff begins to rise from the ocean. Now, when I bring my daughter here, once a year or so, she spends the day carrying stone after stone to our car. She fills our trunk with so many stones that our tires begin to sink into the sand. I sometimes worry we will not be able to leave. I sometimes worry I never have. The day my mother died she walked down to this very spot. This is the closest water to what was our door, though it seemed the ocean was everywhere. She'd already taken her pills, already begun her note. Unlike Virginia Woolf, she didn't fill her pockets with stones, so I imagine her body simply floating on the surface, like a witch—that she could float would prove it.

the story of a million years

AN AFFAIR IS A ROOM where two people can close a door and feel known inside of it. In this room they can have the sense not only of being known, but of being utterly desired— which can feel a lot like love, even if it is, almost always, more complex.

David Huddle offers this:

> When you go into a room with another person and lock the door behind you, you are momentarily free of every principle by which people ordinarily speak and act with each other. How you're going to be— what you're going to say and do, what you think and feel—with that person is entirely up to the two of you. You may legislate as you wish.

One can feel known inside an affair because it is a shared secret. Yet, by definition—and this is the inescapable truth— this secret is based on a lie. Otherwise it has another name, otherwise it is called something else—*an arrangement, an understanding, a compromise.* It is a lie only the other is allowed access to. *If you are willing to share this lie with me then you will know me in a way others cannot.* It does beg the question of whether one really wants to be known at all, or if one is merely seeking to hide.

nick flynn

Adrienne Rich offers this:

> *The possibilities that exist between two people, or among a group of people, are a kind of alchemy. They are the most interesting thing in life. The liar is someone who keeps losing sight of these possibilities.*

Here then is a chronicle of seeking, then losing, sight of all possibility. The day I took my daughter back to my hometown, the day she gathered those perfectly round stones, I was also coming to the end of an affair. How I was able to convince myself that I felt known within that affair is not a mystery— the woman I had the affair with was curious about me, as I was about her. Empathetic, creative, wild—she listened. The mystery is why I didn't feel known within my marriage. Marriage (like life itself) is a daily practice—always shifting, always in a state of becoming. I thought it was one, but it is many—I didn't know that then. Our couples therapist proposes that there must have been a moment of early love, an energy that brought us together. That energy is what we are trying to get back to, he proposes. But for me it is more of a slow build, a slow awakening.

Gradual, like a glacier growing, drop by drop.

Then, like glaciers do, it calved, all at once.

mister mann

Tell me the story of Mr. Mann, my daughter pleads. It's a story I've told her a hundred times already. This, apparently, is what it is to be seven—you can bear to hear the same story, over and over, again and again. Or maybe she has noticed that each time I tell it I add a little more. She wants to know what it was like for me when I was seven; the story of Mr. Mann is what I remember.

This is how I begin:

> *Mr. Mann lived in the woods behind my grandma's, in a house near the cemetery. My grandma warned me to keep away from his house, to not even get close. That if I do he'll come outside with his shotgun and blast me full of rock salt. My grandma told me she knew a kid my age who thought he was clever, got too close, and BAMMO. The doctor had to pick each crystal shard out of his back with tweezers.*
>
> *You're awake the whole time, she said—no painkillers.*
>
> *It didn't kill him? I asked.*
>
> *It's like being stung by a swarm of hornets, she answered.*

I tell my daughter that when I learn rock salt won't kill me I'll end up spending that summer—the summer I'm seven, the summer after our house caught fire—trying to get as close as I can to Mr. Mann.

Or maybe I begin like this:

> *The first time I notice him is in the supermarket where my mother makes donuts. I'd been sent out alone on a mission to the potato chip aisle. He was standing in front of the ones I wanted (Wise), murmuring something I couldn't hear. Long dirty coat, beat-up hat pulled down to his eyebrows, beard gone wild—I'd never seen him, nor anyone like him, before, not in my hometown. I watch as he bends down to the big bags on the lower shelves, as he lifts one to his face, holds it with both hands near to his eyeballs, as if he wants to study it more closely. He whispers something into it, something like a spell, then he puts it to his ear, like it can answer. Then he slips the whole bag, like a big balloon, under his long dirty coat. At this moment he seems, for the first time, to notice me, standing a couple steps behind him. He nods, I nod back. Then he turns, walks down the aisle, right past the checkout girls and the baggers, and out through the automatic doors and into the sunlight.*
>
> *In the car on the way home we pass him, standing on the shoulder by the graveyard, his face turned from us, his hand still under his coat.*
>
> *You see that guy? I ask.*
>
> *Don't stare, my mother answers.*
>
> *Who is he?*

Don't stare.

I don't tell her that I know what's hidden under his coat.

I don't know why I don't tell her.

From then on, I see him everywhere.

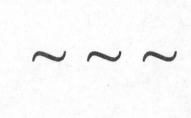

the day before the fire

THE DAY BEFORE THE FIRE my mother wakes me at five to bundle me into the car in the early morning dark. Before her job at the bank she now makes donuts at the new—the first, the only—supermarket in town. Curtis Farms. The mornings I go with her I get the first donut, hot out of the oil. While she mixes the batter I wander the dimly lit aisles, past boxes of smiling athletes, past dented cans of soda. The mornings she lets me sleep in I wake up in the house alone.

This is the first house my mother will buy. It will cost—impossibly—two thousand dollars. She buys it five years after leaving our father, after five years of us bouncing from friends' couches to lousy rentals. An ugly house, sheathed in brown asbestos siding, siding that refuses paint, so we will simply never paint it. If this was Monopoly a house like this would be on Mediterranean, and the rent would be twenty dollars. My mother is twenty-five when she buys it—young, single, beautiful. She has two kids and three jobs and now she (well, mostly the bank) owns a house. A little hand-painted wooden plaque on our wall offers this prayer:

God bless our mortgaged home.

The supermarket opened the year before, on land that had been a field of tenements when we first moved in. A friend of my brother's lived in one of the tenements, but soon enough the workers knocked them all down. After they left for the day I'd wander the muck, ducking between the yellow earthmovers, checking the ignitions for keys. What I would have done if I found a key I cannot say. That afternoon I come home from school to a note on the kitchen table, two dollars folded beneath it:

> *maria's for dinner*
> *I'll be home late*
> *love mom*

This means tonight she's waiting tables at the Ebb Tide. This means my brother and I get to walk the three blocks to the Harbor, to Maria's Sub Shop. I'm six, my brother's eight. I'll get the tuna fish, my brother will get the meatball.

This ritual will become one of my favorite meals.

calisthenics

MOM'S CURRENT BOYFRIEND IS VERNON. He's not always around, but when he is he drills me in calisthenics. Trying to make a man of me, something several of her subsequent boyfriends will also attempt. Vernon teaches me how to crawl on my belly, how to use my elbows to pull myself along the carpet, how to keep my back low so the bullets will pass right over me.

Lower, he murmurs, his boot pressing down on my butt.

I ask him about rock salt. A shotgun sprays hundreds of tiny lead pellets, he explains, opening both his hands in front of my face—his fingers are like flowers, blooming. Same if it's rock salt, he adds. Either one will put a hundred holes in you. The holes pellets poke in you are just bigger, deeper. Rock salt, usually, will only get under the surface. If you stay beyond the blast radius you're safe. If you get caught inside the blast radius you better be fast. Rock salt or pellets, it's best to zigzag, he says, so he has me practice zigzagging.

mister mann

To get to Mr. Mann's the back way you follow the animal path that runs through my grandma's lawn and into the woods. I don't know what kind of animal made this path— *possum? raccoon?* A night animal, an animal I never see, no one ever sees it. The path runs through the woods to a break in a mossy stonewall. It then opens onto the first of three overgrown fields—old pastures, maybe—each contained within other stonewalls. At the far end of the last field, just beyond a collapsed barn, is Mr. Mann's—the backside of the house I've driven past with my mother. She'd pointed it out, told me his name. *That guy you were asking about, that's where he lives.* His windows are dark, curtainless, the shingles so old they look chewed, the lower ones green, mossy. I lie on my belly behind a hillock of grass, I pull myself with my elbows into a swale. I don't take my eyes off his door. I can hear the blood in my ears.

one life to live

GRANDMA SPENDS HER MORNINGS PULLING WEEDS, pruning roses. Afternoons she settles into her armchair to watch her stories—*One Life to Live, As the World Turns*. I'll find her there, stranded before her television, when I make it back from the woods. If the television is off she might be immersed in one of the murder romances she buys from the junk store— she likes her books fat and lurid—she brings home a shopping bag full of them each month.

At five she pours herself a highball.

Turner's Special Blend.

Then another.

Then one more.

The summer after the fire I'll leave a window unlocked in her attic so I can get inside after she passes out. I'll teach myself how to shimmy up the gutter drainpipe to the roof. I'll swipe her menthol cigarettes—Salem—smoke them up in her attic. Then I'll find a whole carton of cigarettes stashed in a wall behind the supermarket. I'll spend my free time smoking them, one by one, hanging off a fence, looking out over the parking lot. I'll imagine I'm perched on the mast of a ship in the middle of a vast ocean. That summer, no land in sight, I'll smoke the whole carton. The smoke tastes good inside me.

Obviously, there's a lot I leave out of the stories I tell my daughter.

the day of the fire

THE DAY OF THE FIRE my mother wakes at five to make donuts. It's Saturday, so she lets me sleep in. Afterwards she has the rest of the day off, so we plan to have a cookout on the back deck. Vernon will grill some sweet Italian sausages he brought us from the city. That afternoon she sets a pot on the kitchen floor between two chairs—beside the pot she drops a paperbag full of apples. She sits in one of the chairs, I sit in the other, facing her. She puts a small knife in my hand, she has a bigger knife in hers. Whoever can peel an apple without breaking the skin will win, but we both know there's nothing to win.

I take my time, make it through the first one without breaking it, a long helix. She concedes, shifts to making the crust, while I finish peeling the rest. Then I mix the peeled apples with cinnamon and butter, dump it all into the pan. She drapes the top crust over it, then I get to puncture the now-bulging pie with a fork, so the steam will escape.

The pattern I make is something like a sun.

wool

My mother's name is Jody. Her maiden name was Draper.

Draper is a name like Smith—it is the name of the thing the people do.

Smiths shoe horses. Drapers sell cloth.

Her father, my grandfather, was a wool merchant, as was his father, and so on, all the way back. What this meant was that we had one bag of wool kicking around our house for as long as I could remember. A paperbag, two blood-red needles poking out from the open top, ten skeins of wool inside. D. J. Waldie offers this: *A loss of belief is what separates us from the much-handled things we grew up with.* This, then, is one of the much-handled things I grew up with—a paperbag, filled with enough charcoal-gray wool for a sweater. My grandfather had given the wool to her when she'd said she wanted to learn to knit.

A sweater.

For me.

When my grandfather was a teenager he lived, for a summer, on a sheep farm in Montana. After the war (WWII) he would go back to that sheep farm, now as a journeyman merchant, to learn the family business: how to grade wool, how much to offer for it, who to sell it to in the factories back East.

His youngest, his daughter (my mother), had been born just before the war. My grandfather held her, he must have held her, at least once, for at least a moment, before he shipped out.

After the war, he came back with this inside him:

> *Knee-deep in the sea, waist-deep, our guns raised above our heads, wading toward the fire. The water slows me, it slows us all. Back home my wife watches over our three children. The youngest, a girl, I hardly know her, I never was able to know her. Something hung between us. Her hand so tiny in mine, her mouth so empty, as if all her teeth had been knocked out by the stock of a gun.*

After the war, as he made his way back and forth to Montana, his daughter grew up—she was what they called in the 1950s "rebellious." My grandfather and his wife (my grandmother) were both drinkers, which limited their parenting skills and options, so at some point it made sense to simply ship Jody off to boarding school. But the first school couldn't handle her, so she was kicked out of that one. And the next, and the next. Think of her as Penelope, weaving her tapestry by day, unweaving it by night, attempting to slow time, to delay the moment she will be forced to decide—delay the moment she will meet my father, get pregnant, and take his name.

He's twenty-seven. She's seventeen.

When I was a boy I'd take the P&B bus into Boston to visit my grandfather in his office. It took about an hour, it cost about two dollars. I imagine my mother bought me the ticket, but that might not be true—I had my own money. Mowing lawns, a paper route. The bus was silver and blue, the *P* stood for Plymouth (where the Pilgrims landed), the *B* for Brockton, which was, and still is, just another broken town to glimpse from the window of a moving bus.

The address of my grandfather's office was Ten High Street. The Draper Top Company. *Top* is a grade of wool suitable to knit. It has been combed, cleaned, spun into yarn. Sample skeins were lined up on a desk in his conference room, and each skein had been touched by his hands, brought here from a ranch somewhere out West—by the end the wool was being imported from as far away as Australia. Some of the wool was sheep-white, some dyed gray, some the black of a black sheep. Each was coiled like a tiny spool of rope, each wrapped in brown paper, a white label affixed to the paper. On the label: the date, the grade of wool, the ranch of origin, all typed neatly out by his secretary. Wool poked out from each end of the neatly wrapped package. Handle a skein and your hands get a little oily. The oil is what keeps the sheep dry, huddled in their field, as rain and darkness fall. The oil is lanolin, it oozes from inside them, we use it to keep our hands soft, it waterproofs our boots. Each strand of wool is lined with tiny hooks, which will hook onto another strand when you roll them together. My grandfather explained this to me, using a finger from each hand to make two hooks—*Like this*, he said.

Wool merchant—even as a child I thought he was out of time, as if he sold buggy whips, or wore a top hat. His father had made a fortune during the wars, back when all the uniforms were made of wool, all the blankets, all the felt that lined all the boots. If you had anything to do with wool you could become rich, and my great-grandfather did. By the time the Vietnam War was winding down, polyester had taken over. Wool would get eaten by moths, wool would end up with holes in it. My stepfather came home from Vietnam with a nylon camouflaged blanket. I claimed it as mine as soon as he left. I'd take it with me camping, which I did a lot. It rolled up small.

When I visit my grandfather in his office the first thing he does is touch whatever shirt I'm wearing, whatever sweater. It's the 1970s, I wear polyester sometimes, we all do—big-collared shirts with cityscapes printed on them, plaid cuffed elephant bells—but not around him. The first thing he'll do when I see him is take a sleeve between his thumb and forefinger and rub it—in this way he will know if the sweater is pure, or a blend.

> In war no one speaks of the ones already down, already on their knees. The ones not yet to the beach yet already fallen into and maybe under the water, under the waves, which will not save them. No one speaks of the man using his gun as a crutch, the man using his gun as a shield, the man who has already abandoned his weapon. None of these men will make it. Empty-handed, hollow-eyed, they wade into the fire, they wade into the smoke. Explosions and fire and smoke, flashes of light which signal a death, then another. Waist-deep, a hundred yards from shore, our rifles above our heads, we piss ourselves empty. We move as one in our uniforms of wool, we move like sheep. Think of it: we are not only moving toward the light, we are becoming light. We all have the same

helmets, we all have the same boots. We are a unit and we move as a unit through the waist-deep sea, into the distant blur.

We always knew that if we wanted to knit anything we could have gotten all the wool we'd ever need from him. If we had wanted to we could have knit eternally, there was no end to the amount of wool we could have had. Unlike Penelope, we wouldn't have to unknit it each night.

What we got was one paperbag filled with a few charcoal-gray skeins—I had picked out the color, it was to be a sweater for me, my mother was going to knit it. We'd moved this paperbag around the house for years, trying to find a place for it, somewhere that would insist. It was on the list of projects but it was the one project forever delayed.

No sense knitting something you'll outgrow in a year, she'd say.

Before there were fields there was ocean. It covered the fields and what drowned inside it became earth. Before there were oceans there were stars, one exploded and the oceans rained down. Before sheep there were wild sheep, they lived in the forests, then men came and captured them—their fleece so matted, it had grown so long, dragging on the earth, thick with brambles. Men invented knives to shear the sheep, invented combs to brush the fleece out, to let the sheep run naked through the fields, which had been coral a million years before . . .

I ask my daughter what she was before she was born.

Nothing, she answers, *I wasn't anything before this.*

My mother's side of the family came over from England to Massachusetts in the mid-1800s, opened a wool mill in Canton. If you go to Canton today the name Draper is still on many buildings. There is still a Draper mill, though this might be other, more distant relatives. I don't know the exact genealogy, nor do I much care. If you go inside the mill you will find machines, looms, invented by my relatives, distant or otherwise, the name DRAPER stamped onto each one. But by the time I came along the bottom had fallen out of the wool market. When I'd go to my grandfather's office he'd be at his desk, looking into a blank screen. He'd be on the phone, talking to another old guy, a crony from the day. *Five hundred skeins of Wyoming grade-A mohair top,* and the crony would take it off his hands. On the walls of his office were etchings of sheep, Currier & Ives, men in top hats lining the pens. This was the world, and then it changed. In this way all the money that had passed down to him from all those wars slipped through his hands.

This is the truth about the war: my grandfather came from money, so whatever combat he saw was all in his mind. He was a Seabee, construction battalion. His job was to supply the ships with food, with clothes. His war was far from the bombs, the fires, the blur. He wasn't at Normandy, he did not storm the beach. He did not run into the fire. He came home from his war intact (mostly), and there was his daughter, now almost six, her hand still so tiny in his. Remember: before she defied him, before she brought shame, before she went off with one of the men who dug ditches in town, she was a child.

Then, just as my grandfather was leaving his wife for his secretary at the Top Company (*Meet me in Reno, love, and we will begin our new life*), Jody got pregnant. Years later, when I am twelve, my mother will remarry (Travis, the Vietnam vet) and take his name, which left us, her and me, with different names. Four years later, after Travis leaves, she'll go back to her father's name, her maiden name.

Again, think of my mother as Penelope.

Now think of her name as her tapestry.

Perhaps, by unweaving it, she was trying to return back to the source.

The wool for my sweater waited for years in its paperbag. Those two red needles waited. My grandfather would ask about it, at our monthly lunches in his mansion, the mansion he inherited from his father. I'd wear one of the plaid Pendleton shirts he gave me for Christmas each year. That way he wouldn't even have to feel it to know it was pure.

But still, he touched it.

Currier & Ives on the walls.

A bookcase lined with porcelain sheep.

A wine cellar.

Ten crackers on a plate.

My mother, he demanded, needed to make something with what she'd been given, before she'd be given more.

Eventually my mother picked up the needles and began. She must have taught herself—maybe she read a book. I can remember the sweater, I wore it constantly—charcoal-gray, cable-knit on the front—but I cannot see her sitting still long enough to make it. I cannot remember when it was new, but I remember the elbows, blown out from wear, the sleeves stretched long. One sweater, out of all those sheep, all that wool. All those factories, all those wars. It was, by the end, little more (again) than a pile of yarn.

After the elbows were blown out I put the sweater in mothballs. I'd only pull it out for our monthly lunches with my grandfather, which, near the end, were more like every other month. This was the uniform I wore to his house, until the end. That chemical smell of mothballs hung off me as I sat in the mansion—could everyone smell it or just me? By then I was drinking—once he even offered me a beer, but I didn't stop at one. *Look at what I have made*, my mother might have uttered, *from the scraps you have offered.*

purple room

VERNON WAS A CARPENTER. After the fire my mother hired him to renovate the house, so the insurance money—at least some of it—went to him. Years later he'd tell me it was hard for him to hand her the receipts—two kids, three jobs . . . Besides, he was married, so it was hard for him to ask her for much.

The night of the fire he was sleeping over, so maybe it was the two of them who woke me.

It will take months after the fire for the house to be livable, and in those months we will have to find somewhere else to be. We will sleep on the couch of a waitress my mother works with at the Ebb Tide. We will end up spending a lot of time at my grandma's, the nights my mother works, so that we're not always underfoot at her friend's.

Most of Vernon's time will go into renovating her bedroom, as if this is the only room that matters.

Dark purple carpet, light purple walls.

Purple pillows, purple sheets.

The one window with its gauzy curtain, the one lamp with its purple shade . . . even then some part of me understood. The rest of the house will remain a grayish beige, but a purple glow will now seep from the edges of her closed door.

Inside, an empty coffee can (Maxwell House) holds her

tip change from the Ebb Tide—purple quarters in the purple light. The old can melted—*good to the last drop.*

The room, when finished, will always smell of chemicals, the purple wall-to-wall off-gassing. My mother will later confide in me that it wasn't the shade of purple she wanted, not how she imagined it, but it wasn't worth telling Vernon.

what you can't hear

THE CHILD LOOKS BACK at the window of the room he's just fled, each pane now filled with sparks, each spark one of his toys—*monkey spark, Matchbox spark, yo-yo spark*. It was the smoke that woke him, nothing else. When he woke, the air was smoke, but now it is studded with sparks.

Lightning bugs, he thinks—*my room is filled with lightning bugs*.

Mom in her bathrobe, Vernon in his boxers. Sparks swirl around their words.

The child wants to run back inside but he cannot.

His feet sink into the lawn.

The trees reflect the house now, their leaves illuminated from below, like the palms of gospel singers. *When does a lightning bug become a firefly?* he wonders.

Years later he will be in bed beside a woman and he will tell her about the fire—*We all made it out okay*, he tells her, his eyes still studded with sparks. But when she reaches for him it is with hands of smoke, as if the smoke were a cloud in his lungs, as if too much dark lived there.

Outside his window it's that tree again, singing.

What you can't hear is the light caught in each bud.

What you can't hear is the leaves inside each bud.

synecdoche

In the film *Synecdoche, New York*, Philip Seymour Hoffman plays a theater director who is spiritually adrift. In the scenes I remember he wanders a huge, crowded warehouse, rehearsing his latest play, which is described as *a celebration of the mundane*. He ends up working on it for years—many assistants, many sets—while his life steadily falls apart around him. His days are spent casting it, rehearsing it, directing it, writing it—but he has lost track of the plot. Or else he is still searching for the plot, but it is, as is often true, elusive. The part I always remember is when his wife takes their five-year-old daughter on a trip to Berlin. Once they are gone he quickly loses track of them—can't get them on the phone, can't connect.

The play has overtaken his life.

It has become, like a Borgesian map, the size of his life.

What I always remember is that, a few months after his wife leaves him, he opens a fashion magazine and sees a photo spread of his daughter—suddenly, impossibly—now a tattooed teenager. That always unsettled me, how quickly we could lose track of those closest to us.

How quickly we could lose track of ourselves.

I haven't seen the film in years, but for some reason I think about it a lot.

Grammatically, a synecdoche is a word where a part stands for the whole.

It is a type of metonymy, which is a subset of metaphor.

If you call a businessman a *suit*, you are in the realm of synecdoche.

Today, before the house was awake (I am using "the house" as a synecdoche), I was listening to the radio. A man was talking of the Talmud, how each word in it contains the whole, how it reveals the interconnectedness of all things. This concept weaves through most spiritual thought—Native American to the Mahabharata to Buddhism. Poet Stanley Kunitz distilled it to this: *Touch any strand of the web and the whole web trembles.*

I rewatched *Synecdoche, New York* last night. It was hard to see Philip Seymour Hoffman again, to remember how great he was, before heroin took him out. Until I saw it again, I'd forgotten the other reason I remembered the film. In a recurring scene, Hoffman's character enters the house of a lover—the house is, for some reason, always on fire. Smoke fills the rooms, wisps of flames in the corners, but no one seems worried, or to even notice. I had remembered Hoffman standing in a room that was ablaze, but upon rewatching it I see it is more subtle.

Just smoke, just wisps of flame.

I'd also forgotten that the film starts with a voice-over of a Rilke poem—*Whoever has no house now will never have one.* One could say that by taking that lover, Hoffman's character was entering a house on fire, or that he was burning down his own house—either of those images would also be in the realm of synecdoche.

supermarket

I have the key, my mother thinks. *I let myself in.*

Inside, she moves through the darkness—past the leaky AC, past the red stools that barely spin, past the baskets of jelly already lined up, past the cup stuck to the counter by a ring of yesterday's coffee. The bakery is through that doorway, behind the lunch counter. Three switches light it up, the rest of the supermarket remains dark.

She thinks:

> *I'm here to make donuts. Donuts are my job. My purpose. My kids are still asleep at home, maybe just now waking. I told them I'd be gone when they woke, I left a note. They don't complain, they know how to be alone. I'm alone here, thankfully alone. The only other light comes from the meat department, way in the back. The light in the meat cooler never goes out, I don't know why that is. Yesterday's meat, one day closer to* manager's special.
>
> *Eggs in their cartons, butter in its block.*
>
> *I pull on the apron, fire up the oil, the sun not yet risen.*
>
> *I make a pot of coffee.*
>
> *If I follow the recipe taped above my station, everything will work out. Two bags white flour, two gal-*

lons whole milk, a dozen eggs, a bag of sugar. By now I know where everything is. I cruise the dim aisles, filling my cart. Sometimes I imagine I'm in that tv show—Supermarket Sweep—where you get to run through a supermarket, pushing a cart, throwing in whatever you can grab. You have two minutes to spend as much as you can. If, at checkout, your total is the highest, you win. Most go straight to the meat department, that's where the money is.

No one goes for the donuts.

Sometimes I can imagine filling a cart, pushing it out to my car, then driving off into the sunset. Or sunrise. Instead, I break the eggs, I open the bags, dump it all into the stainless mixing bowl. Press the green button, the metal paddles slowly turn. The manager showed me everything. Wait until your spoon can make a dent in the batter. Use the spatula to fill the extruder. Wait until the oil in the vat reaches 380. Press this button. Everything is taped to the switch. It's not that difficult.

Yesterday's paper is tucked under the counter. While the dough mixes she pours herself another coffee, turns to the science section:

Does time have a direction? When you pour cream into your coffee it swirls around—the cream doesn't tend to funnel up out of your cup and back into its carton . . .

Does time have a direction? Is it really just one day then another?
She thinks:

> *My youngest is six. I swear to Christ some days I
> feel like I'm six alongside him. Some days now I can
> barely see over the steering wheel. At that moment
> I'm shorter and smaller and have to reach up for
> things. And there we are, reaching up for the milk,
> and there it goes, all over the floor, and no, it won't
> funnel back up into the carton, not ever. That's the
> second law of thermodynamics, that's* entropy. *I
> remember that from science class, from when I was
> going to be Madame Curie. I was going to discover
> something, and what I discovered would, even as
> it saved everyone else, kill me. And now here I am,
> more Lucy Ricardo than Madame Curie, my hand
> reaching up to the switch. No one's even looking. The
> thermostat reads 380 now. Here we go. I pour the
> batter into the extruder, I set the timer, I stand by the
> vat with my spoon, the big one full of holes. Once the
> batter begins to drop into the oil I need to be ready.
> It only takes a minute and a half—I know when each
> is done by the shade of brown it turns.* Ready, set. *I
> love the hiss of the dough as it hits the oil—roiling
> in the agony of becoming, someone once said. How
> magical it seems, that a little circle of goo will form
> into this and not into something else. Sometimes I
> imagine letting the ring of batter drop, then simply
> watching it. How long would it take? Until what?*

Maybe I'll never take them out, maybe I'll let the whole vat fill up, until they tumble out onto the floor. Let them go past being donuts to become something else. We can all be something else. But here I am. I don't want to remember waking up at four, I don't want to remember the ice on the windshield, scraping it while the car warms up. I don't want to remember the mornings the car refuses to start, or the look on my kids' faces when I come home and they'd woken again without me. I don't want to remember their cereal bowls in the sink, and the days I just can't bear it.

The darkness of the supermarket, beyond all this, waits for her. The janitor comes in to mop the floors. Before he comes she can hear the rats eating their way through the fruit in the produce aisle, the aisle farthest from her. A cabbage falls to the floor. The rats, startled, squeak and scurry away. After the floor dries the produce guy will walk down the aisle, wheeling a trash bin, tossing out anything with gnaw marks in it.

the carpenter, the fisherman, the insomniac

She thinks:

> I remember the day the first man tapped on the window before the supermarket was open. Stopping by for an early donut. Then came the others—men who worked late, men who worked early, men who didn't work at all. The carpenter, the fisherman, the insomniac. At first all they wanted was a donut.
>
> It sometimes feels like a fairy tale—men, tapping on glass, looking for something. I'm asleep in a glass coffin. One of them could be the one to waken me.
>
> But am I the princess, or am I the witch?
>
> In the fairy tale the princess stands on a stool and pours batter into a machine. An extruder drops a ring of this batter into the hot oil below. It bubbles, it roils, it changes color. It looks like it hurts, the princess thinks. Her stepmother locked her in this room when she was a child, promised she would unlock the door once she made a hundred (a thousand? a million?) donuts. There is no escape. Each donut ends up in the display case, all day the firemen and the carpenters come, and one by one, or by the bag, these donuts go.

Tomorrow it will all start again.

Here's a word I remember from school: bewilder—1684, Anglo-Saxon, *from verb* to wilder, *to lead someone into the woods and get them lost.* To wilder—*that's the job I want, I want to be a* wilder. *Maybe I already am. Maybe that's what I'm doing to the men who come to the window looking for an early donut: wilding them.*

the cop

I remember how it felt, the first time the cop tapped his nightstick to the glass. I remember wiping my hands on my apron. I remember how I could not not go to him—he was, after all, the law.

I remember how he stood there, not smiling, not speaking. I opened the door. Like the others, I had to invite him inside.

I remember three days of this, three dark mornings, maybe four, until I grew to wait for him. I remember his nightstick, the sound of it, how it glistened, until I grew to want it. I couldn't stand there long—the donuts, after all, were browning.

My kids, after all, were sleeping.

The rats, after all, were hungry.

In the end he was just another worker.

In the end my job was simply to bewilder him.

diorama

ANYONE DRIVING PAST, OR SITTING in their car in the parking lot waiting for the supermarket to open, can look right in. Inside it is still dark, as dark as outside. The light on the coffee maker glows like the lit end of a cigarette. Your mother passes back and forth to the bakery through the lit doorway. The men who sit in their cars, they can't help but notice her beauty, a smudge of flour on her forehead. The mornings you go with her you wander the dim aisles, lit only by the slowly brightening sky. As if it were all yours, as if you will never go hungry. The produce is covered each night by a thin white shawl, as if what is below is dead. The meat, wrapped in plastic, sleeps in little black trays. The mornings you go with her you wander past the cereal you are forbidden to eat, past the soda you are forbidden to drink. *That crap will rot the teeth right out of your head*, your mother tells you. *I spent a lot of money for those teeth.*

scratch

A STRANGER, ONE DAY, KNOCKS on the window. She goes to the sound, like she always does. When she opens the door it is as if she knows him, as if she's been waiting all this time just for him.

Oh, she says, it's you.

A yellow smell, sulfur eyes.

Are you here for a donut? she asks, though she knows that's not really why anyone comes to her door.

I'm here for you, he answers.

She takes a moment to consider this—such honesty is new.

Tell me, child, he asks, what is it you want?

She wipes her hands on her apron. She can't remember ever being asked that question.

I want to go back, she tells him.

Back, he repeats, stepping inside.

He is standing very close to her now.

You smell so good I could eat you, he says.

She looks at her hands, white with flour.

You do know that house is killing you? he murmurs.

My house?

It's little more than a bundle of thorns. It was never meant to hold you, not while you're still young, still alive.

She nods slowly.

I don't feel so young anymore, she says.

No one is, he answers.

He puts an arm around her shoulder.

I know a way you can walk away from it, he offers.

Walk away? she repeats.

I know the way back, he says.

A lit match appears between his fingertips.

One match and you can go back.

Now the match is between her fingertips.

Here on earth it's gravity that makes fire flow like water, he explains. Elsewhere fire is a perfect orb. Elsewhere children can live inside these orbs, like fireflies.

Fireflies, she repeats.

supermarket

THE AC OFF-FLOW RUNS DOWN this once-clear tube, empties into a stained bucket. The bucket stinks, but it's not her department. The red stools, lined up like boyfriends. She spins one as she pulls on her apron. And here's the basket of jelly, each sleeping in its little airless tub.

August. The mornings have begun to stretch out. Crickets weave their legs into sound in the tall grass that lines the parking lot. The leaves make that slight death rattle sound that signals the end of summer, but hasn't it only just begun? Not yet dawn, darkness pushing on darkness. It lives beyond the wall of glass. An airplane passes overhead, but you cannot hear a single person breathing inside it.

That one light on in the back.

She thinks:

> *I don't want to remember this moment, when the idea first took hold, like a match being slowly pulled across a flint. It's not a thought I want inside me, but there it is. One by one the grains ignite, like this thought, growing bigger. So many words, so many ideas. It sometimes feels like my head is full of flames. When did I think that having a kid would solve anything? Did I ever think that, or did I just wake up one day and find myself here?*

After that moment, it was as if each of my eyes
was a flame. I had to stop looking in the mirror.

The first donut is ready. She will catch it with her spoon, let the oil drip off it, move it to the rack.

insurance man

ONE MORNING, IT'S THE INSURANCE MAN tapping on the glass.

She thinks:

> I don't want to remember the day, a week or so later, that I went into his office, even though he'd said, specifically, Stop by anytime. I don't want to remember sitting across from him, or the short dress I was wearing. I don't want to remember asking how much I'd get for a fire, right after asking about a flood, but we both knew it wouldn't be a flood, that no flood was coming. I don't want to remember his smile, or his hand in his lap, the one with the ring. Stop by anytime, he said, after we'd signed the papers, even though I already had.

> I don't want to remember him in line at the bank, the day after the fire. I don't want to remember his smile, how different it was—I hope everyone's okay, he said tightly. Something about him reminded me of how, after a few drinks, my mother would light a cigarette, then swing the lit match lazily back and forth in the air beside her.

> No matter how long she shook her hand it wouldn't go out.

> Whatever happens, I will not become her.

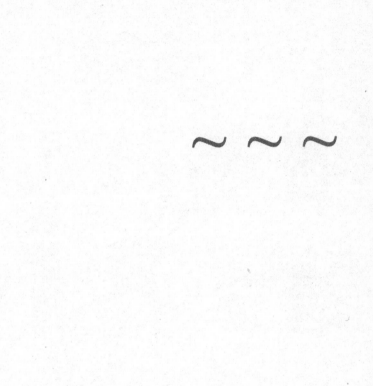

penelope sunshine

THE YEAR BEFORE SHE BEGINS to ask me about Mr. Mann, each night I will lie beside my daughter at bedtime to tell her a story. It's a story that's been unspooling for the past several months. A never-ending story, though one day it will end. It takes place on an island of monkeys, the hero is a girl the same age as my daughter. John Cassavetes once proposed that when a character can't find his way home, that's where the story begins. So that's where I began:

> *Penelope Sunshine wakes up on the Isle of Blue Monkeys. She didn't know how she had gotten there.*

Penelope was from a circus family. Her act was to be shot out of a cannon. But one day her brother put too much gunpowder in and she was shot clear across the ocean. My tendency, I soon discover, is for the story to go dark, and quickly. For the monkeys to turn authoritarian, for Penelope Sunshine to be lost in a maze, for the queen to be taken over by her witch nature. I have to always remind myself that I am making this story up for a six-year-old. Penelope never dies in these stories, but she has to figure out a way to prevent her darker impulses from taking over.

The thing about having a kid is that, inexorably, one thing transforms into another. This moment will become another moment, which will then become something else.

Mark Epstein, writing about the nature of reality, offers this:

> *Everything is burning then, not only with imperma-*
> *nence and pain but also with bliss. The vision of one*
> *leads to the knowledge of the other . . .*

When telling the story to my daughter, I need to remember the bliss. Yet, as the story unspools, it becomes harder and harder to bend the story toward the light. Barabas, the strongest of the monkeys, has declared himself king. He essentially enslaves the other monkeys, demanding they bring him one coconut each day, which leaves them hungry. Barabas hoards these coconuts in an underground room. Occupy Wall Street had ended only a year or so earlier, I'd taken my daughter there several times. It allowed us to talk about the gap between the rich and the poor, about how some folks have so much by taking it from those who already have so little.

In order to end the story, I have a typhoon hit the island:

> *The worst storm in years, the whole island flooded.*
> *As the water rose, each monkey climbed his or her*
> *tree, right up to the green leafy top, and the water*
> *followed them up. Each held on to one coconut, for*
> *if the water didn't recede then at least they would*
> *have something to eat. Barabas tried to carry all the*
> *coconuts he had collected from the other monkeys,*
> *but he couldn't hold them all, and in the end he had*
> *to let go of all but one, just like everyone else. The*
> *rains lasted for forty days, and the water now came*
> *right up to the bottom of the leaves, so that each tree*
> *looked like a green island, floating in a vast sea. The*
> *monkeys could yell across the water to each other,*

but none of them could swim. They could see Bara-
bas, alone on his own green island, but he no longer
seemed so large. In the rain Barabas looked like just
another monkey. As the rain continued he began to
grow even smaller. At first his pants seemed a little
loose around his belly, but then, a few days later, they
slid right off him. He was soon no bigger than his
coconut, and then he was no bigger than a blueberry.
Finally a drop of rain came and he stepped inside it
and was carried away.

In the end, the rains subside and the water recedes and the
monkeys rebuild their homes. In the end, there is no longer
a king. Barabas, in the end, is everywhere—in all the water
that falls from the sky, inside each coconut. When the world
flooded, Penelope managed to get aboard a boat. The boat
washed up on a strange shore, which turned out to be her
home. A poster nailed to a tree said that the circus was coming
to town, so she knew she would soon see her family again. On
the Isle of Blue Monkeys, a monkey left a little jar outside his
hut—in the morning it was filled with dew, tinged blue. When
he held it up to the sun it looked like a tiny Barabas inside—
sleeping, smiling.

The end.

run

Run, my mother says, shaking me awake.

Only a voice inside my dream, but the dream's already
sinking.

Breathe through this, she says, reaching into the dark water,
pressing a wet cloth over my mouth.

I don't know which is thicker—the dark, the smoke,
or the voice in my head. *We have to get out, now.*

I still can't see, but I run.

I remember tumbling down the stairs into the thicker
smoke.

I remember my body, how it knows not to breath.

medea

VERNON IS STILL LIVING with his wife, staying over at our house the nights he can get away. A Catholic—the affair, his three children, have all begun to weigh heavily on him. One night, he tells my mother they need to end it, that it can't go on. Our love is a type of madness, he tells her. But my mother, she doesn't want to let go. Over the next weeks and months, breakup becomes a refrain. My mother becomes desperate to hold on to him.

He doesn't tell her that he's begun seeing someone else.

In Euripides's version, Medea is betrayed by Jason—he plans to leave her to marry Glauce, a princess. Medea, a barbarian, is good with potions—in Jason's quest she'd put a dragon to sleep so he could slay it. Medea had left her own people to be with him, and by now they had two children together. *I am the mother of your children. Whither can I fly, since all Greece hates the barbarian?*

Vernon did leave my mother, but he also left his wife. For what it's worth, he left his wife for a woman with the same first name as my mother. Then, out of all the places he could have gone, Vernon moved his new wife into a house just down the road from us. The thing is, except for the nights he'd slept over at our house, before this he'd never lived in our town.

I found a letter, after my mother died, hidden in her bureau, written to her (I imagine) by Vernon. It seems she is pregnant, or worried she is pregnant, and in the letter he is trying to talk her down, gently, to tell her that everything will be all right. *Take a nice hot bath tonight*, he writes her, *you will feel better in the morning.* It is unclear why she saved this one letter.

Let's not panic until we know more.

It turns out she wasn't pregnant, or if she was she *took care of it*. Maybe this was when the idea first took hold, to find a way to start again. Maybe that would hold him to her. Jason had offered to keep Medea around as a mistress, but she had other desires. My mother had other desires as well. To enact her revenge, Medea poisoned Glauce and her father (Creon), and to further punish Jason, she killed their two sons.

My mother, clearly, is not Medea.

That I am writing this proves it.

I think about them now, the men in my mother's life. By the time I understood (or thought I did), she seemed fiercely independent, unwilling to let any man in too close. After Vernon, she had a series of boyfriends, but none stayed around that long, none lasted. When I was thirty-five I looked up each one of them. I went to them, asked each how they met my mother, how they found out she had died. I distilled my passion into these two questions—maybe, at that time, this was all I could handle. *The truth must dazzle gradually.* This was how I found Vernon, now living alone in a gated community in Florida.

canopic

FIRE CONTAINS TIME. Fire is time converted into light. Fire takes trees and allows you to read other trees. The book in your hand was once a tree, now you hold it up to the tiny fire inside the light bulb so you can read it—the words, then, hopefully create another fire, in your mind.

Gaston Bachelard offers this:

> *Fire is the ultra-living element. It is intimate and it is universal. It lives in our heart. It lives in the sky. It rises from the depths of the substance and offers itself with the warmth of love. Or it can go back down into the substance and hide there, latent and pent-up, like hate and vengeance.*

In one version of the night our house caught fire I'm carried outside in my pajamas, left to stand across the street on the lawn of the neighbor we'd never met. In another version my mother shakes me awake with a word, and the word is *RUN*. Or maybe she simply yells, *GET UP*, from the bottom of the stairs. Or maybe she doesn't say a word, maybe the house is silent, maybe it's the smoke that wakes me. In all versions there's a lot of smoke and I escape by running through it. I'm left on the lawn to watch the shadows of the flames on the nearby trees.

In my mother's version it was raccoons that started the fire—they upended the hibachi, and the coals, still glowing, spread out across the porch. For years this was the story because it was a story that had an ending, even if it ended in flames. As a story it was, at least, *comprehensible.* The days leading up to the fire we'd watched them, every night from our kitchen window, come to raid our garbage pail—we were amazed by what they could do with their hands, which seemed so much like our hands.

We knew what they were capable of.

Joan Didion offers this:

> *We have learned to freeze the shifting phantasmagoria which is our actual experience . . .*

Let me begin again:

> *One summer night our house catches fire. I'm six. I have to run through the smoke to escape the flames . . .*

A thousand and one times I've told this story. *Why?* Because it happened. Because I escaped. Because it involves fire, and firemen, and sirens. Sometimes (still) this story starts with just me, barefoot in the next-door neighbor's yard, looking back at the house we've just tumbled out of—all I can do now is watch as it burns.

Phantasmagoria—I need to freeze—make sense of—the story of being six and running through a burning house. I need to contain it, like a firefly in a jar. If I don't contain it I don't know if I can move away from it, and if I can't move away from it I don't know if I'll ever believe that I made it out in one piece.

Yet here I am. I stand before you. Intact. Whole. Holy.

Everything that lives is holy.

In earlier versions of the story it was a perfect summer day. Mom and I made an apple pie. Vernon grilled sausages on the back deck. Then, after we'd all gone off to bed, after Mom (I guess) tucked me in, the raccoons came and tipped the hibachi over.

The coals fanned out across the wooden planks.

It was then only a matter of time.

But it was always a story, like all stories, that came in several jars, like those jars the Egyptians would use to hold the entrails of their dead—*canopic*—lungs in one, heart in another. Liver in one, spleen in another. You've seen these jars—empty now, the organs long desiccated—in the Egyptian wing of the Brooklyn Museum.

the happy jar

WHAT WAS IT WE USED to chant into the mirror each morning, in what used to be called the "New Age"?

    Every day, in every way, I'm getting better & better.

What is it we chant now? Eduardo Corral offers this:

    Some days, when I catch my
    reflection in a mirror,
    I think, Someone has hurt this animal . . .

Years later, when asked about my childhood, I'll say, *It was happy*—for years after the fire this is the only jar I'll open. *THE HAPPY JAR.* If I tell someone about my mother and how she died, the next question is, often, How did you survive? meaning, How the hell are you so well-adjusted?

    Well-adjusted? I'll think to myself.

    But I'll answer, as I always answer, I felt love, I knew my mother loved me.

    I'll answer this way even after (*shifting phantasmagoria*) I learn that she'd set the fire herself.

I'm thirty-five when I track Vernon down. Thirty-five is (perhaps) the age when one can approach the past without believing it will annihilate you. To annihilate means to reduce to nothing, to ash. Vernon laughs when I mention the raccoons. *That house was a real shithole,* he says, *all it needed was a match.* He tells me she had something going on with the local insurance agent, that she got the house insured for more than it was worth. As he spoke I both knew and didn't know what that meant. In that moment one jar became two. In one was the fire, in the other was my mother setting the fire. In one I was happy, in one I'd survived, in the other I never made it out of that house. One meant she was clever, resourceful, that she knew how to get over. One meant she was broke, desperate, and a fire meant we would get a nicer house, and we did. The other meant something else, something I wasn't ready to take in, not fully—it's entirely possible I'm still not ready, but here I am.

Whole. Holy. Full of holes.

question

FIRST THERE WAS ONE JAR, then two, then many—as a story it began to multiply.

In this jar is a plan—the plan is that the firemen will come in time. Only they didn't come in time—she had to make her way through the now-burning house to my bed, shake me from my dream of smoke. I was a fish gasping for water on a tile floor, a balloon rising from a child's fist (*balloon* rhymes with *raccoon*), the endless inside of the vacuum cleaner, and the memory of how it smells.

QUESTION:

> Did she really have a plan? Was the plan always to save you? Was she always going to wake you with a word— *RUN*—or did that word somehow find her?

QUESTION:

> Which came first: the fire, or the idea of the fire? The sound of the alarm, or the alarm itself? Think of the power contained in one match, the power to go back to before there are children. She was still young, she could start again. She lights one match and knows the firemen will come, she knows one match can make the whole station light up with sirens.

QUESTION:

Why do you think she bought a house sheathed in asbestos across from a fire station?

QUESTION:

Is it possible the word *RUN* was only in her head?

Here's a passage from a poem I wrote before I knew, at least on a conscious level, that she'd set it: *You can run / back into a burning house, sinking ships // have lifeboats, the trucks will come / with their ladders, if you jump // you will be saved . . .*

smoke

AFTERWARDS, SMOKE BECOMES MY DREAMS—I can breathe in it. Afterwards, all bedrooms are thick with smoke. Smoke tastes good, afterwards, inside me. Smoke is a blanket, smoke asks a question—the question is, always, *Why not?*

In *The Body Keeps the Score*, Bessell van der Kolk offers this:

> *Trauma by its nature drives us to the edge of compre-hension . . . Sooner or later most survivors . . . come up with what many of them call their "cover story" that offers some explanation for their symptoms and behavior for public consumption. These stories, how-ever, rarely capture the inner truth of the experience. It is enormously difficult to organize one's traumatic experiences into a coherent account—a narrative with a beginning, a middle, and an end.*

Afterwards, if asked, I'll tell you that it's possible—likely—that my mother set our house on fire with me (and my brother) asleep inside it.

Through fire everything changes.

The worst part is that I'll tell you all this with a smile.

When we want everything to be changed we call on fire.

We got the money.

this god

EACH OF US IS PART of a whole, a thread in the fabric, a one among the many. Yet, together, simply by looking, we create what some would name "God." I don't believe in God, but I believe this (which I took from the wall of a 12-step meeting I call home): *Days pass and the years vanish, and we walk sightless among miracles.* I believe Nina Simone: *I want us to wake up while we still have time to wake up.*

Quantum physicist Fred Alan Wolf offers this:

> *Somehow, when you consciously observe something, a possibility becomes real and "out there." And the evidence seems to be pointing to the conclusion that there is only one true observer, one mind in this whole universe—a Mind of God, so to speak— for which each sentient life form plays a role making up what Jung may have deemed the "collective consciousness" . . .*

Some nights this is what I believe: this God was there as my mother took her spoon and swept the glowing coals, one by one, toward the dried-out shingles, the shingles she'd already doused with lighter fluid. This God was both the wind that fanned the flame and the flame itself. This God saw the flame, the flame that was itself, and did not kill it. My mother crouched on all fours in the dark—*yes*, like a beast. Each window that looked out upon her was, *yes*, this God. There are words that only find themselves in your mouth once you are in the presence of the thing itself. This God was *spark*, then *smoke*, then *flame*. Then, finally, *beast*. The animal of her, this God, it walks up the stairs, to where you are sleeping, it moves in its robe of smoke, to lean into your face, to kiss your eyes shut. The only question it asks (the only question it ever asks) is, *Are you ready?*

Imagine the night, then, before she steps out into it, how it fills her hands. She thinks the lines on her palm are a map, but they are, still, only this God. In her palm is a box, inside this box ten infants sleep, their little red hats pulled down tight to their heads. Using her body as a shield, she runs a match across her teeth. A neighbor, looking out her window at that moment, sees a thing hunched over. Is it trying to get inside, but inside what? Then something bright, then a flash, then a spark. This God is the neighbor's eyes, then this God is the neighbor's wondering. This God is the neighbor who never picks up the phone, who simply pulls the curtain shut . . . My mother, on all fours now in the moonlight, lights match after match on her teeth. You know how this God works, how it whispers into you, how it offers the answer to all your problems. Sometimes the answer is *jump*, sometimes the answer is *fire*. This God, it whispers that if she were alone she could start again—this is what it always murmurs. This God wants you alone in a room without doors or windows, it wants to fold you back into the earth. If you had gone to her at that moment she would have leapt on you, tore at your eyes, your eyes which, after all, created her.

police report (imagined)

At approximately 1:30 a.m. the residents of 32 Brook St.—a mother with her two young sons—entered the fire station, which was directly across the street from their house. The sky was clear, cloudless, the stars bright. The mother, Jody Flynn, wore a robe; the boys, barefoot, wore pajamas. The man who accompanied them, wearing only boxer shorts and a t-shirt, declined to be identified. The family entered the fire station and encountered three firemen on duty, playing cards. One of the sons yelled, *Our house is on fire.* One of the firemen simply nodded toward the bell on the wall and said, Pull it. The youngest child pulled the bell at 1:34 a.m. and the firemen threw down their cards and pulled on their boots and slid down the pole. The fire truck started and the door opened and the sirens swirled and the truck drove loud right past the house. The mother and her sons went back down the stairs, crossed the street, and stood on their lawn, waited for the fire truck to return. Their house was already full of smoke, all their windows glowed, yet no flames were visible.

you can't always get
what you want

OUR QUANTUM PHYSICIST NOW WONDERS if the universe isn't made up of separate particles, and if each particle doesn't, in fact, contain the whole. Our quantum physicist has observed that under certain circumstance these particles are able to instantly communicate with each other, regardless of the distance separating them. It doesn't matter whether they are ten feet or ten billion miles apart. Einstein used the word *spooky* to describe this phenomenon. One possible conclusion is that the universe is a hologram. *If we try to take apart something constructed holographically, we will not get the pieces of which it is made, we will only get smaller wholes.* There is no answer, we've come to believe, unless they are not only *made* of the same thing, but *are* the same thing. Think of a film of a match igniting, how you can play it endlessly, run it forward and backward—the flame comes alive, the flame returns to the tip. A Buddhist would say that the flame was always in the tip, sleeping, just as the flame was always sleeping in your mother's eyes. Can we ask her, can we ask anyone, not to see? She will, at some point, have to drop the match, as the flame creeps closer to her fingertips. The box of matches will need to be brought back inside, put back in the drawer by the stove where it lives, beside the can opener and the spatula.

Now you're seven, now eight, now nine—you watch her twirl her hair obsessively as she drives you to another nowhere. She wraps a lock of hair twice around one finger, pauses, scratches the coil three times with her thumbnail, repeat. The same song drifts from the window of each car you pass—*You can't always get what you want*. Your mother twirls her hair. Ten years later she'll be in a strip joint snorting coke with her gangster boyfriend. Five years after that she'll be dead. She'll make a hole in the fabric of the universe but this time (maybe now you're too big?) she won't try to push you through it. This time she'll leave you on the other side, alone.

x

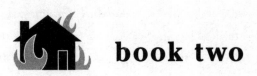

book two

ladybug, ladybug, fly away home
your house is on fire
your children all roam

tape recorder

By Christmas, a few months after the fire, our house is in good enough shape to move back into—some work to finish, but good enough. More gifts than usual appear beneath the tree that year, maybe because of the insurance money. Usually we get some socks, a notebook, colored pencils, a sweater. Maybe a board game. And—always—the latest Beatles album. But this Christmas there's more, a lot more. What I remember is a tape recorder, a small reel-to-reel, which seemed ridiculously extravagant—I knew Santa hadn't brought it. I don't remember asking for it, I can't imagine I would have. I remember feeling guilty, opening it—we'd been living off my mother's tips since I was born, and this must have cost a small fortune. I knew, though, to pretend to be excited. I hugged my mother, thanked her. I set it up then and there, then went around the room with my little microphone, from my brother to my mother, interviewing them. It had a little handle so it was easy to carry. Here's a young lady, say something for our radio audience about Christmas. And tell me, young man, what is your favorite present this year? Young lady, could you tell us your favorite Beatles song? Could you sing it? I hit the rewind button and there is my mother, answering my questions, singing, *I'm not what I appear to be . . .*

I put it away after that, in my desk, and never used it again.

Vernon, of course, wasn't there—he was with his real family—though he had left a present for both me and my brother.

Mine was a sweatshirt, Snoopy dancing across it, his happy dance.

thin ice

THE BROOK OUR STREET IS NAMED FOR flows behind the firehouse, creating the low point between Brook Street and First Parish Road. I cut through the firehouse parking lot to get to school each morning, cross over a little culvert, watch the brook flow beneath—with the spring thaw it'll flow heavy, but by August it'll be a bare trickle. I still don't know where the brook starts—its *source*—maybe it wells up from underground, but doesn't everything?

As the brook gets closer to the harbor the land around it becomes a saltmarsh. The marsh then bleeds into the harbor, then the harbor opens into the Atlantic. But none of this is known, not yet, not by me. Even if I did know, it wouldn't be the important thing. The important thing is that every winter the firemen flood the swampy area before the culvert so that us locals can skate on it. At this point this is as far as my world goes.

The brook our street was named for was called *satuit* by the Wampanoags, who were no longer apparent by the time I was born.

No longer apparent. As in *gone.* As in *annihilation.*

The town itself was named after the brook—Scituate, pronounced sit-*choo*-it.

My grandmother remembered the Indians, as she called them, from when she was a girl, knocking on her back door, hungry. They wore rags, she said, like hobos. Gone, without a trace, but for the names of things—*satuit* meant *"cold brook"* in their language, at least that's what we were told.

But, of course, by then there was no one to ask.

The winter after our house catches fire I'll pull my pal Stephen Donovan out of the ice behind the firehouse—he'd tested the THIN ICE sign, fallen through, his head bobbing up and down from the hole his body had made. Arms waving, his voice getting smaller, I grab a hockey stick, slide it out toward him on my belly, tell him to just hold on.

The fire had taught me how to do that.

Fire taught me everything.

six baby mice

No one's paying much attention, so when school ends I'm free to wander. It's the summer after the fire. If my mother was out working the night before, or on a date, I'll wake up at my grandma's. At some point each morning I'll announce to my grandma that I'm heading into the woods. The woods are vast, I might as well have said I was diving into a bottomless pit, but it seems enough for her to know this. *Don't get in any trouble*, she'll say, or *Be careful*, or *Watch yourself*, or something equally grandmotherly.

Dinner's at six, she'll say.

One morning, along the path, I find an old bottle dump. I line the bottles up on a rotting board and pitch rocks at them. Underneath the board I find six tiny baby mice, squirming in little tunnels carved in the dirt. The mother is nowhere to be seen. I watch them for a while, then lay the board back down.

Every day that summer, I drag myself a little closer to Mr. Mann's. From a safe distance, I begin to study him.

No screens, his windows shut tight.

Frogs in his pond, no wind.

Sometimes I see him poking around in his fallen-down barn, or feeding his broke-backed horse, but mostly he's a ghost.

~

Years later, I'll publish a book of poems—*Some Ether*—my first book. The first poem in it is called "Bag of Mice." It is one of the few poems of mine to come from a dream—I simply transcribe it:

> *I dreamt your suicide note*
> *was scrawled in pencil on a brown paperbag,*
> *& in the bag were six baby mice. The bag*
> *opened into darkness,*
> *smoldering*
> *from the top down. The mice*
> *huddled at the bottom, scurried the bag*
> *across a shorn field. I stood over it*
> *& as the burning reached each carbon letter*
> *of what you'd written*
> *your voice released into the night*
> *like a song, & the mice*
> *grew wilder.*

I wrote this poem before I found Vernon in Florida, before he told me my mother had set our house on fire. It may seem strange, but I swear I never consciously linked my mother's suicide with the fire, and I am reluctant to do so now. It would feel reductionist, to make it easier (if that were even remotely possible) to explain her suicide. Did it weigh on her, what she had done when she was younger, when she was desperate for a way out? Fire appears in each of my books, but then so does a donut—that's the way the (my?) subconscious works. In the town I grew up in—Scituate—which was the same town both my mother and father grew up in, oblivion was the air we all

nick flynn

were breathing. From what I hear, the air there is still thick with it. *You're not from these parts, you don't know what our twilights can do.* I have a friend who, like me, grew up in Scituate, but thirty years later. You might hope things had improved, that my people had figured some things out in the years since I left, but you would be wrong. Too many of his friends from high school had died—ODs, car wrecks, suicides—my friend fled into the desert to escape it. Something is in the air, in the water. It would be easy to simply name it alcohol, but that too would feel reductionist. Alcohol is, likely, a symptom of something deeper. Whatever you call it, whatever it is, this malaise, it makes my people keep going back to the well, over and over, long after they know it is destroying them, and everything around them.

When I finally dragged myself to therapy at the tail end of my twenties, a period of my life that, even at the time, I described as *fleeing as if it were a house on fire*, the therapist took one look at me and pronounced me alcoholic. I looked at him; my friends and I had—jokingly, proudly—called each other "alkies" since we were fifteen.

I know that, I said. *That's not why I'm here.*

It means you can't drink, he pointed out.

He was clearly confused.

It means I do drink, I gently clarified. *That's what alcoholics do.*

I'm not going to waste my time with you, he sighed, *unless you stop.*

treefort

IT'S THE SUMMER AFTER I escaped our burning house, yet each night I have to return to it. I never know if my mother will, or will not, be there. It's been renovated, yes, but it still smells like smoke—it'll smell like smoke until we move out a couple years later. A purple glow now bleeds from the crack beneath her bedroom door, but what does that mean? Does it mean she left her light burning? (*unlikely*). Does it mean she's alone in there, standing before her dresser? (*unlikely*). In the top drawer she keeps her empty pill bottles, the pills for her migraines—*Fiorinal. Darvon.* Yellow plastic bodies, white plastic hats, each wearing a white label, each label with her name typed out neatly upon it. Take by mouth, they say. Take with food, they say. Why she holds on to them once they are empty she cannot say. To keep track, but of what? In case it gets out of control, she thinks, but what is "it"? She cannot fit any more bottles into the drawer, so several are now lined up on the top of the dresser, also empty, also waiting, but waiting for what? Is it possible they could all be refilled one day, that she could haul them to the drugstore and explain to the pharmacist that there must have been a mistake, that they all came to her that way, empty?

That summer I get it. What I need to do is build a new home, beyond anyone's reach. I need to find a ladder so I can climb a tree and live in it. I need to be closer to the stars, which we all know are dead. I like how each one can fit into my eye. I'll lie on my back on a branch up there and look at them, invisible from below.

Me, not the stars.

I'm invisible from below.

In my grandma's attic I find a book of Addams Family cartoons. I don't find them scary—I find them helpful, like blueprints. Pugsley builds a car out of a coffin. Wednesday builds a rack in their basement. Gomez has a huge picture window put in so the family can all look out over the graveyard. It helps me understand: a ladder is just some boards nailed to a tree. I can do that.

On the edge of the fields that lead to Mr. Mann's I find the perfect tree. Even from the ground I can see two branches that run parallel. I'll lay a few boards across them to build a floor. I'll drop a rope from it to haul the rest up. I'll build a ladder to the sky, and in the topmost branches I'll rest. I can climb as high as I like, I can just keep going, no one will tell me where to stop.

Mr. Mann's barn had fallen years ago. Ferns, grasses, now sprout from it. Some boards are mossy, scattered about, waiting. I drag myself toward it, across the last field, I crawl on my belly. At the edge of the barn I crouch on all fours, I don't take my eyes off Mr. Mann's door. Nothing moves. I reach for a plank, I take it and run. Then I crawl back, later, for another. This time I wait for Mr. Mann to be gone, I wait for him walk into town, to shoplift some chips, I guess. I drag all the wood I might need to the edge of the barn, so it'll be easier to grab. I find a broken hammer and a tin can full of rusty nails. I find a small blue door with a rusty handle and the letter *M* carved into it. It's the door to a chest now gone. I take it to make my own door. I am building a house, I need a door.

The *M* once stood for *Mann*—it now stands for *Mine*.

Before my treefort I was left to wander, to pick my way across unexplored ground. Before my treefort I was little more than a blind baby mouse hiding under a rotting board, waiting to be found. Before my treefort I'd wander the fields, penned in between stonewalls, like a sheep. I never looked up, I tried to walk softly, without making a sound. The leaves beneath my sneakers could sound like gunshots, like pockets of water inside green wood popping to life in the flames. *Pop.* I'd stop, stand stock-still, listen. No one was coming. After I found the tree I knew I could escape. I saw a ladder rising into the sky before there was a ladder. Here's what I don't say: I built my treefort too high, dizzyingly high, from the earth. If I fell I wouldn't just get hurt but would likely die. Scattered beneath the tree was a broken stonewall, broken open by the tree growing out of it. It would break me if I were to fall.

Here's a story I came up with, lying on my back on the platform I built:

> Once upon a time there was a bunny who found himself alone in a field, chewing off the tops of wild carrots. A boy was walking along the path, but the bunny didn't see the boy. The boy lit matches and let them fall from his hand, leaving a trail of small flames behind him. The bunny saw the flames jump onto the dry grass and rise up behind the boy like a specter. The bunny ran and ran. He ran so far that he

got lost and couldn't find his way back to his burrow. Years went by, the bunny never went inside. One day he met another bunny, and she tried to lure him inside, but part of him would be left, the part he left behind in the fire, and he didn't want to abandon any part of himself.

wig

ONE NIGHT, TWO YEARS BEFORE THE FIRE, my mother appeared to me unrecognizable. She was supposed to pick me up at my grandma's, but when she opened the door she was not my mother. She arrived when my mother was supposed to arrive, she drove my mother's car, she held out her arms and called my name, but she was not my mother. My mother was a brunette, and this woman was a blonde. It was just a wig, but I was too young to understand. I ran and hid behind the couch and she laughed and my grandmother laughed and I heard them laugh. Now I understand she must have been on a date, now I understand she was "done up." She'd always joked that one day she'd give me back to my real mother (you know the way parents joke). She'd always joked she wouldn't be around forever—I thought forever had arrived.

After that she kept her wigs on her bureau, each one balanced on its styrofoam head. Totemic, like an altar to possibility. She could be anyone, her pill bottles scattered at their feet. After that I never knew who would come home at night. Without a wig she was simply my mother, with the wig she could be the mother I was going to be given back to—my real mother.

Years later, in a junk store, I find it—a styrofoam head. As a kid I'd destroyed so many—beaten them with baseball bats, kicked them around the house. I'd use one as a dummy in my own bed, to trick my mother when she came home after midnight. I'd hide in my closet, waiting for her. Just as she'd lean in to kiss me I'd jump out. Ha! She'd jump a little, then laugh, then tell me to get back in bed. She'd rub my back until I fell back into my dream. After she quit making donuts, she was always there in the morning when I woke up, even if some mornings, the mornings she didn't have to get ready for work, it was hard for her to get up. I knew to let her sleep in, those three styrofoam heads watching over her. Each glowed white in her curtained bedroom, like the bulbs of certain flowers, hanging under the crust of the earth. Inside each bulb is an endless flower, one after the other, year after year, they never stop coming. Like tuning a radio, turning the dial, how it finds a song from nothing, from air, each styrofoam head was there to take up the space left behind when she was gone. When she was gone they would talk to me. This is how I remember her— a head without eyes, a face without a mouth. I could melt each one with a lighter and huff the fumes. I could submerge each one in gasoline and each would turn to napalm. Once, when she was out, when I was afraid she wasn't coming back, I drew eyes on her styrofoam heads.

What did Saint Francis say? *What we are looking for is what is looking . . .*

Later that night she came home, blurry and cigarette-smoky. She sat on the edge of my bed.

I won't be around forever, she whispered.

She thought I was asleep.

Get ready, she whispered.

Run.

buster keaton

A FILM STILL IS TACKED to the wall above my desk. In it Buster Keaton walks in front of his soon-to-collapse house, a hammer in one hand, a saw in the other. He looks over his shoulder toward us, away from the house. The look on his face, as if to say, *I'm not really a carpenter*, which is obvious. As if to say, *I'm pretending*, which is what we do. As if to say, *I've never lived in a house*, which is possible, growing up as he did on the vaudeville circuit. As a boy, Keaton was the punching bag of his family's act—onstage he was knocked over, kicked, whacked, pummeled. At one point he had a suitcase handle attached to his side so he could be thrown farther. He found that if he made no response the audience would laugh louder, so he made no response. In this photo, his house is impossibly crooked—the porch already fallen, the roof will not keep out the rain. The windows, more parallelogram than rectangle, will never open. But, even if imperfect, it is, still, his house. He has built it, likely for a woman, a woman who, I imagine, doesn't even notice him, until the end, of course, when she will see how hard he's been trying, and with so little, all along.

500 miles

WHEN SCHOOL ENDED FOR THE SUMMER, the next day I'd be on a bus to go to camp. Camp Daniel Webster. Overnight the school bus became the camp bus, every morning my mother would send me out to wait for it. *Take care*, she'd say. She'd packed my lunch—an apple, a bologna sandwich, chips. A devil dog, sometimes. I could buy milk at camp, and an ice-cream sandwich. We'd sing "500 Miles" on the way there— *Lord, I can't go back home this-a-way.* I remember the camp as huge and wild and fun, but it was likely very basic. My mother was working every day at the bank, waiting tables weekends at the Ebb Tide. She could, at most, afford a month at camp—the other month of summer I was free to wander the woods.

The camp was in Marshfield, the next town over. We'd file off the bus, walk past the tetherball courts, past the path to the .22 range, to gather on the edge of a circle in the grass. Once we settled down, Coach Anderson would come out of the house in his shorts and high socks, his crewcut and whistle, and march to the middle of the circle. We'd all watch as he'd silently, slowly load his pipe with Borkum Riff. Once it was lit, he'd launch into an inspiring story—a fable, a parable, an allegory— something with a moral at the end. One about a carpenter who built a house for a rich man, using the cheapest of materials, pocketing the money he saved. The carpenter knew that within a few years—soon—the windows would leak, the doors would creak, the faucets would drip, and the chimney would crumble. Even the nails he used were inferior, and would, eventually, dissolve. The carpenter resented the rich man, which made sense to me, though I didn't know why. One day, when the rich man came to inspect the work, he had a surprise for the carpenter. All along he'd been planning to give the house to the carpenter as a gift, for him and his family to live in. The rich man was grateful for all the work the carpenter had done for him over the years. The carpenter, stunned, could only say, *Thank you*, even as he remembered the windows that would leak, and the doors that would creak, and the nails that would (somehow) dissolve. *Thank you*, was all he could say. Coach lit his pipe again, to give us time to take it all in, to chew over what it could possibly have to do with us. *Was I the carpenter? Why did I hate the rich man? Can nails really dissolve?* We considered it, cross-legged in our required t-shirts with the camp logo on them—a green circle made out of the words CAMP DANIEL WEBSTER. In the middle of the circle a . . . *what? a bird? a feather? a bow and arrow? a gun? a quill and a scroll? a Pilgrim shaking hands with an Indian?* I really cannot remember.

On Mondays, after his story, Coach would announce Camper of the Week, and one boy (were there girls?) would go up and get a white felt badge pinned to his t-shirt. It came with a free ice-cream sandwich every day for a week. Camper of the Month came with a bigger badge, but I forget what came with that . . . an ice-cream sandwich plus something else . . . but what? What could Coach offer that could possibly be better than an ice-cream sandwich?

whirlpool

ALONG WITH THE GUN RANGE and the tetherball courts, the camp had a field where we played capture the flag, an archery range, and a murky pond with tin boats to row among enormous croaking bullfrogs. And a pool—blue-bottomed, white-edged—where we'd learn to swim. As a camper progressed up the aquatic food chain, from pollywog to frog to seahorse to turtle to seal to dolphin to shark to whale, he also got a series of badges, white paint on felt (again), this time cut into the shape of whatever level of creature was attained.

Before entering the pool we first had to change into our swimsuits in the spidery barn. Then we'd march across the lawn to the pool. A counselor, twirling a whistle on a gimp lanyard, would line us up along the edge. Maybe twenty of us pollywogs, the lowest of the low, were told to lower ourselves in when we heard the whistle, but not to submerge. We were to line up with our hands on the edge, and to not let go. Pollywogs, we didn't even have legs, not real ones, not yet. To graduate to frog we had to do three things—blow a hole into the surface of the water, make an alligator growl (a mouth half in, half out sort of gargle), and submerge our heads for a couple seconds. It seems so easy—blow a hole in the surface of the water? When was I not able to do that? Yet I have a memory of clinging on to the side, the blue vast and deep beneath me.

If I let go I will slide beneath the surface, I will vanish into it. I bend my face to the water, my face comes up to meet me. *Blow*, the counselor orders, so I blow.

Next came frog.

Frogs have legs, real legs, which means we still have to hold on to the side but now we have to kick—*flutter-kick*, they call it, but it is more like we are running as fast as we can, only without bending our knees. *Kick kick kick*, knees and elbows straight. Hours pass like that, excruciating hours.

Once we'd flutter-kicked ourselves to nothing, the counselor blows his whistle, yells, *WHIRLPOOL*. Fifty, a hundred of us, we line up in the water along the edges of the pool. The counselor blows his whistle again and we all turn to our right, place a hand on the shoulder of the kid in front of us. When we hear the whistle again we begin to march, slowly at first, like worn-out prisoners being forced back into the salt mines. One hand on the wall of the pool, one hand on the shoulder in front of us, the water starts moving, slowly at first, then a little faster, then faster, then even faster, until our bodies begin to be carried along, until our feet no longer even reach the bottom. *WHIRLPOOL*. If you try to stop you find you cannot, and when you stumble you are still carried along, tumbling now, head-over-heels, not even a prisoner any longer, more a pebble now, more the salt than the miner, dissolving.

What would the quantum physicists—locked in their labs, eyes to their telescopes—say about this? Would they say that each kid is a particle? Would they call the swimming pool a black hole? Our quantum physicists warn that the particle we are looking for, the one some call God, could one day be responsible for the destruction of the known universe, if they ever find it. They also say that *the universe we experience is just one of a gigantic number of worlds. Some are almost identical to ours while most are very different.* Does this mean that somewhere, at this very moment, a hundred children are still (forever) caught in a whirlpool of their own making?

black hole

THAT SUMMER, THE ONLY THING I WANT, the only thing any of us seem to want, is to be caught—lost—in the black hole of the whirlpool. To both create it and to become it. Soon, whenever we have free time, we all line up around the edges of the pool, turn in the same direction, and start our slow march. I like how my body becomes just one of many bodies, I like how, after a while, I can't even touch the bottom. I like losing control, how the whirlpool picks up my feet, how it carries me along. It's a small storm, it's the eye of the hurricane, with no way out once you're inside. If I close my eyes I can still feel myself being carried along by—dissolved by—something that is bigger than me. I close my eyes. I see the fence that separates the pool from the wilderness, I see myself pressing my face against it, my eyes pressed to the space between the boards, looking at the whatever that is happening beyond it . . . on the other side of it . . . in the place beyond the . . . in the place I cannot see. Maybe whatever is happening on the other side always happens at that same time every day, or maybe whatever is happening just keeps on happening. Maybe what is happening is beyond knowing, but then what moment isn't always, essentially, beyond knowing?

dead man's float

ONCE WHALE IS ACHIEVED, the final swimming lesson is *rhythmic breathing*, also known as *the dead man's float*. This, we are told, is the most important skill to know, the one thing that could actually save us. At some point in our lives, we are told, we will find ourselves in the middle of a dark ocean—no boat in sight, nothing to hold on to, not even a piece of a lifeboat. At that moment we will need to conserve our energy. To swim will be impossible, without knowing which direction we should even start out in, without seeing land. All the strokes we'd spent the summer learning—*the crawl, the sidestroke, the butterfly*—none of it, in the end, will save us. To practice the dead man's float we hang lifeless, our arms making a ring in the surface of the ocean. We lower our heads into this ring, exhale underwater. Then we raise our faces up, slowly, just enough for the next mouthful of air.

The swim coaches were right. Many mornings since then I've woken up in that dark sea—no shore in sight. *The real death is being dead while alive*. This sea, when it speaks, it uses my voice. It murmurs, *Take care*. It murmurs, *Get ready*. It murmurs, *Watch yourself*.

the field

THE CAMP BUS DROPS ME off at three. I leave my grandma in her chair, watching one of her stories, and head into the woods. *Come back in time for dinner*, she says, her sauce simmering on the stove. I've pilfered a box of matches (STRIKE ANYWHERE), it's in my pocket. Only it doesn't stay in my pocket, now it's in my hand. I don't have a plan. *There but for the field, surrounded by stones.* I'm lighting the matches one by one, letting them drop, as I follow the path through the field. *There but for the grass, dry now as straw.* I leave a trail of dying flames behind me, like a trail of breadcrumbs. I flick the white tip with my fingernail. Flick it on a rock, flick it on the zipper of my fly. I even flick it on my teeth, like I'd seen in a movie, so the flame starts inside my mouth and the sulfur fills me. Then the sound of wings somewhere. *There but for the path, no grass grew upon it.* When I turn, the field is on fire behind me—the flames have wings, like Satan. Then and at once I'm in the middle of it—it moves that fast, it surrounds me. It flares up then dies, it jumps tuft to tuft, thick with a language I don't understand. In that moment it's as if I were born knowing one thing. What I know is that it will never stop, that the flames will jump the stones, that the woods will burn, that the houses will fall, unless I do something. I wouldn't have jumped into the flames and with my sneakers stomped it all back into blackness, every last spark, but for the voice, tiny inside, that whispers, *Don't run*.

one week

UPDATE: I TRACKED DOWN THE film the Buster Keaton still is from—*One Week* (1920). After watching it I see I had it all wrong—the woman in Keaton's film loved him all along. It opens with the couple getting married, rice thrown at them as they leave the church. The car that drives them away from the wedding has two signs hanging from the back: JUST MARRIED, and GOOD LUCK, YOU'LL NEED IT. As a gift, the newlyweds have been given a build-it-yourself house—it comes in a series of boxes from the Portable House Co. The directions say: *To give this house a snappy appearance put it up according to the numbers on the boxes.* The film chronicles the week it takes for the couple to assemble the house. But a jilted suitor scrambles the numbers, and so the house ends up being put together wrong. Misshapen. Even so, the wife paints two black hearts on the side, an arrow piercing them both. Once they move in, more problems arise—ceiling leaks, doors lead nowhere. During a housewarming party a windstorm shakes the house from its foundation, then blows it in circles, as if it were floating on a giant lazy susan. Keaton runs outside to stop the house from spinning, as the guests inside tumble, their hands in the air, and his wife spins around and around on a piano stool. As the storm ends, one old man looks at his watch as he makes to leave, tells Keaton he had a lovely afternoon on his merry-go-round. In the end, they discover they built the house on the wrong lot. As they attempt to move it, it gets stuck on a railroad track, and an oncoming train finishes it off. Keaton and his wife walk off, hand in hand, seemingly content to be, once more, without a home.

polaroid

A BOY IN TWILL OVERALLS stands against a brick wall, holding a Polaroid up to his face. In the Polaroid the boy stands against a brick wall, his arms down by his sides. We know it's a Polaroid because it has that tab that Polaroids have, the one that allows you to pull it from the camera. The boy holds it gingerly, his fingertips on either side of it, as if it is still a little wet, as if it is not yet set. It covers his face, except for the hairline, which is cut at a rough angle.

His haircut reminds me of a film still of my wife (she's an actor) from *I Shot Andy Warhol*. In that film she plays Valerie Solanas, the deranged woman who shot Warhol. In the film-still her hair is all choppy bangs, cut at the same angle as this boy's. Her mouth is tight, her eyes tight. She aims a gun out of the frame, either at Andy or at me.

I saw *Warhol* when it came out, though it would be years before I'd meet her. We were both with other people then—now we are with each other. That we have made it this far deserves some praise. That Warhol didn't die that day deserves some praise.

The last line of the last book I wrote is this: *Here's the future, tapping my younger self on the shoulder, saying, I will be here for you, if you can find your way to me.* The book is called *The Reenactments*—it chronicles making another book

I wrote into a film. I wrote a book, then it was made into a film, then I wrote a book about making the film. A snake eating its own tail. Ouroboros.

The future tapping my younger self on the shoulder was my wife, who played someone I worked with in a homeless shelter when I was younger. What I didn't say was that by the time I wrote those words I was at the threshold of an affair. What I didn't say was that the affair started, in some ways, the moment the filming began, the day I saw my mother's suicide being reenacted by Julianne Moore. Julianne writes the note we hear in voice-over.

I threw myself in the ocean, she writes.

I began an affair, I didn't write.

swifts

THE WORLD IS ABOUT TO END, so my wife spends part of each day looking at birds. Birds are a prophecy, an auger. We are both worried and not worried about this. The world has been ending since Blake wrote his apocalyptic visions (*O thou art thyself a root growing in hell*). The world is always about to end.

My wife stands in a field and looks into the sky and listens. I join her. It is overcast. I can't hear a thing.

Swifts, she says, pointing.

I look up. Only clouds.

There, she says. Way up.

Then I see one, the V of its wings. Then I see another, then another. So far away, so tiny, but the more I look, the closer they come. No, the more I see. Hundreds now. Now I can hear them, gathering.

Chimney swifts, my wife says. It is nearly sunset and these swifts will need to go in for the night. Why they do this I do not know. Some birds (pelagic) simply float on the surface of the ocean for the night. Some roost on branches, sometimes a whole tree is nothing but bird. Some nest on the ground, you need to be careful where you step. Some don't sleep at all, but just fly and fly and fly.

I have learned all this from my wife.

A chimney must be nearby, she says. So we get in the car and drive, to the nearest factory or school, somewhere that will have a chimney large enough for all the swifts in the sky to roost in for the night. An elementary school is two blocks away. It is summer, so the chimney will not be in use (by winter, when the chimneys will be in use, the swifts will have migrated farther south). We get out of the car, look into the clouds.

Look, my wife says.

Swifts, gathering.

I can hear them now, using echolocation to feed on mosquitoes.

Wait, my wife says.

At last light the swifts, suddenly and all at once, become a black rope in the sky and in less than a second this rope coils and pours itself into the chimney.

In less than a second the sky is silent.

I have never seen anything like it.

upside down

THE WAY THE SWIFTS GATHER and pour themselves into a chimney reminds me of that photograph of the boy holding that Polaroid in front of his face. I forgot to mention that he holds it upside down, so his head is aiming straight into the earth. It reminds me of how cicadas live underground for seven (some for thirteen) years, feeding on the roots of a tree. Until some signal lets them know it is safe for them to come out. Then they emerge and climb the same tree they've been living under and devour all its leaves and call out to find a mate and then give birth and die. Then their offspring drop back into the hole in the ground the parents only recently emerged from and it starts all over again.

Swifts need to find a chimney each night at last light.

At sunrise they will emerge.

Look, my wife says. She is standing beside me.

For my wife and me the world ended a long time ago. That is how we found each other. Our fathers were both the men in our towns others would either laugh at or avoid. Madmen, fools, drunks. It's been a hard year for us. A hard few years. I haven't been a good husband in many ways. I am so close to her now our arms are touching. She can feel my body tremble. She knows that some part of me is not safe, that some part of me could destroy her, if she let it in. It hangs outside our bedroom door, it breathes in the night. My hands give off sparks and she moves away from them. It is as if the thoughts in my brain were coming out of my fingers.

I look up at the sky. Clouds mutating.

I have been with my wife now longer than any woman I have known, except for my mother. When I met her I was like that boy holding that Polaroid up to his face, as if to say, *This is me*. I thought I could hide, I thought I could mutate. I wanted to be seen but I was upside down. When you looked at me this is what you saw. It was a mask that looked just like me, only wrong. What was I afraid of, what would happen if she actually saw me?

model t

A BLACK MODEL T, the kind of car with running boards, the type of car you'd see in a Buster Keaton film, is parked between the fallen-down barn and Mr. Mann's house. A tree, impossibly, has grown up out of the middle of it, pushing a hole in the roof, its trunk as thick as my leg. A maple tree, the leaves in the fall are as red as flames. Word is that Mr. Mann, once he found out that he had to register and insure his new car, parked it there and simply never moved it again.

This is one of the stories I tell my daughter:

>One day, early August, I crawl right up beside the Model T. I'm as close to Mr. Mann's house as I've yet dared. I try the car door, pull it open, climb inside. I sit behind the wheel like I'm the driver, the tree like someone in the backseat. The seats torn up. I chauffeur the tree for a while, talk to it over my shoulder. Here is the famous fallen barn, here is the hermit and his shotgun, until the door to Mr. Mann's house swings open with a bang. I sink low, hold my breath—if he sees me in his car I'm a goner. I peer over the back of the driver's seat, my face hidden by the tree. Mr. Mann is in his doorway, his beard all bushy and white and wild,

looking out across his fields. A moment later he steps
back inside, pulls the door shut behind him. I count to
ten, slide out of the car, and run back across the field.

nick flynn

the end of the affair

Most nights she comes back after midnight. Some nights she doesn't come back at all. Always on her way elsewhere, always another job.

One night, as I wander our dark and newly renovated house, I see my mother's car in our driveway. The car is dark except for an intermittent glow from the tip of a cigarette—it comes & goes, with each in-breath.

I can see the shadow of the man she's talking to beside her. I know it's Vernon—he always smells of smoke. I'm in a dark window, so they can't see me.

His arm around her, like a wing. The tip of her cigarette glows. They sit in the car and fill it with smoke. Each word, each murmur, glows like the tip of her cigarette, like a buoy in a vast sea.

The radio plays "Be My Baby"—everyone loves that song.

They cannot see me at the window, except in the moments between her in-breath, when the tip of her cigarette goes dark—

in these moments I am forced to look back into a darkness that swallows us both.

At times each word must be no more than a whisper, a dial that can be tuned.

Whoa oh oh oh oh

A match illuminates the whole diorama, I see her face briefly as she lights another cigarette—without a cigarette she will float out of the window like a balloon. Without a song on the radio her lips will stop moving. Without a hand on her thigh she isn't there.

The gearshift is on the steering column, if she pushes it forward the taillights will come on and it will mean they have made their plan & the grass behind them will glow like fire. If the car door opens & the interior light flicks on then I will find her in the morning, asleep in the purple room. I will let her sleep in.

For one brief moment she looks straight through all the darkness, back at me in the window.

I blur my eyes, like she taught me.

After tonight, Vernon will go back to his wife, and we won't see him again, not like this. My mother will then lock herself inside their purple room for a few weeks, with her migraines & magazines—purple will become the color of pain.

Purple pain sounds like *purple rain*.

I remember rubbing her feet after he was gone.

I remember when she came home from work with
a run in her stocking, how we'd race it all the way
up her thigh.

That summer, once a month or so, we have lunch at
my grandfather's house (*the big house*) on First Cliff.
Boys in their cutoffs line up along the bridge that
leads from our house to his. We stop at the drugstore on the way so my mother can pick up her white
paperbag—it's stapled shut, as if a queen had put her
wax seal upon it. It lay on the seat beside her. Inside,
the bottle is childproof, but the boys who leap from
the bridge would know how to open it. Just push down
& turn, the same way they push their whole bodies
down & corkscrew into the water below.

scroll

ONE DAY, WHEN I'VE CRAWLED almost to his fallen barn, the door swings open. Mr. Mann steps out into the sun, squints out across his field. I flatten—I don't move, I don't breathe. His right hand is still inside his house, either on the knob or on his shotgun. I can't tell if he's seen me. Part of me tries to calculate how far rock salt could sail, whether it would be dispersed enough by the time it found me, whether I should make a break for it or sink lower into the grass. He steps out and pulls the door shut behind him, looks around one more time, like a dog sensing something in the distance. Then he turns and walks around to the front of his house and up the driveway to the road that will take him to the Harbor. I watch until he vanishes into the trees, then I run—not away from his house this time, but toward it. I want, just once, to look inside. I want to see what it is like in there. I try the door but it is locked. A dark window to the left of the door, I look around for a board to lean against the shingles beneath it. The barn is full of boards, I find one and drag it over. I climb it and press my face to the glass but the glass is filthy, so I try the window. It gives. I open it a little, tilt my head to see in through the crack, but inside it's dark, so I open it wider—wide enough to put my head inside. Once my head is in, my whole body tumbles in behind it until I am fully inside. I stand up, press myself to the wall, hold my breath, waiting for my eyes to adjust. When I can see, the first thing I do is look around for the shot-gun, but I can't find it. I am in a long dusty hallway lined with shelves, and on the shelves are many small cardboard boxes—maybe fifty boxes—each about the size of a roll of quarters or a stick of butter. I open one. Inside is a scroll—when I unfurl it I see it is a column cut from a very old newspaper. Closer, I see it is a story, one that would appear each week—a serial-ized story—last week's installment sewn to the week before with thick black thread. Like stitches. The one in my hand is Dicken's *Nicholas Nickelby*, and the date on the top is 1838. These are his books, I realize. I've heard of Dickens, and my name is Nicholas, so I put it in my pocket. There is also a cigar box full of wire-rimmed glasses, the type that John Lennon wears, so I take a pair of these as well. I start to worry, I know he can come back any moment, so I close the window and let myself out through the same door he'd used. I drag the board back to the barn, and run the scroll to my treefort, to examine it more closely. *There once lived, in a sequestered part of the county of Devonshire, one Mr. Godfrey Nickleby . . .*

When I tell my daughter this story, which I do over and over the summer she is seven, she always ends by asking where the scroll is now. It is possible I still have it, stored away in a box in some attic, though that is unlikely. Over the years almost everything that could be lost has been lost. I will search for it, I promise, and if I find it, it is hers.

woodcock

MY WIFE IS ON A retreat. Birds are migrating. She calls to tell me that at dawn she went to a dark field to watch woodcocks fly into the air to mate. She was told to lay her body down in the exact spot from where the woodcock alit. It is promised that when it returns it will, calmly, land back on her chest.

Is this the type of trust I want, to simply lie in a field, to wait for something unexpected to return? As a child what I saw made it clear that if I could simply get to the next day it would all be okay. Beyond the saltmarsh, beyond Mr. Mann's, I had no sense that to simply be in the day itself could be enough.

When my daughter asked this was all I could remember—the saltmarsh, Mr. Mann's—the only places where I felt safe to breathe. Maybe my wife lying on her back in the darkness, waiting for that woodcock to return, is like that as well. To place ourselves where something bigger, something more mysterious, can happen.

Birds copulating above us in the fading darkness.

I told my wife the story of Mr. Mann a few days after I began to tell it to my daughter. It would still be months before I'd reveal the affair. It seemed a way for us to get closer, for us to know something about each other, to reveal some part of myself that she didn't know. I was a child. I spent time in the woods, I didn't know why. At that moment I didn't connect

Mr. Mann to the summer before, to the summer our house caught fire. I'd told my wife about the fire, I must have, but I likely told her the cover story. That we all made it out okay. That we got the money. I don't remember her saying that it was wrong, what my mother did. But it seemed she understood.

In telling this story now I feel like I am postponing the inevitable. I keep going back to my childhood, telling myself it is the source, but maybe I am simply, again, not able to stay in this moment. My wife is in the bed beside me. She tells me about her weekend. About the woodcock. There is a vortex of words trapped inside me. I am afraid if I start to speak I will not be able to stop.

Pull on a loose thread, the whole sweater comes apart.

asbestos

THE WORD *ASBESTOS* DERIVES FROM the ancient Greek, meaning "unquenchable" or "inextinguishable," which seems the opposite of how we think of it. Our house on Brook Street survived the fire, in part because the asbestos shingles repelled the flames—here is the house, here are the flames, kept apart (almost) by asbestos. Asbestos makes a house seem constant, as if nothing will take it down—not termites, not fire. Can I say my mother knew it would never burn? Can I say she intentionally bought a house sheathed in asbestos across from a fire station because she knew it (us) would have a chance (or two) of being saved?

One theory of the universe is that it is expanding faster than we ever believed, that it isn't constant. If we shine a light into the universe it will go on forever. It will never find an end, because the universe isn't a bottle, where light can find the wall and bounce off it. Its structure is what it does—it expands, so the light keeps moving farther and farther out, into this endless expanse. Maybe this explains why I can never come to the end of this story, why it always seems there is more to ask. The universe is expanding, the house is on fire. No matter how long I look at it, I don't know where fire goes, if it does not go back inside the match. I don't know where the child goes, if he does not go back inside the mother. The house I grew up in is now filled with strangers, the furniture now holds no emptiness shaped like my mother. The youngest fireman is still on the lawn, his hose still in his hand, left to look for sparks that might still be alive. Once the flames are dead, once the sparks are silent, he will declare the house empty, but he won't check that closely. He won't see I'm still huddled inside. He won't see my mother, still standing by the stove, waiting for the pie to cool. We all pass right through him.

mister mann

THAT WINTER MR. MANN lies in his bed beneath all his blankets as the snow around him deepens. He lies in the dark with the windows gone white, his breath like a song hangs above him.

This is what my mother told me:

> Mr. Mann hadn't paid his bills—not gas, not electric, not oil—so he got shut off. They unplugged him. He'd only lived with electricity for a few years, and now they killed him, by taking it away. Con-Ed bills filled one corner of his room, unopened. His obituary would say he was ninety-three years old. His obituary wouldn't say that the electric company had killed him, but everyone in town knew. We killed him because he was poor.

querencia

MY MOTHER SELLS THE HOUSE on Brook Street when I'm eight. *A new start.* The Brook Street house needs a new roof, and without a carpenter boyfriend it is simpler to move. Besides, it still smells of smoke. My mother finds a house on Third Cliff, closer to the ocean, a (barely) converted summer cottage. It turns out (*surprise surprise*) to need a lot more than just a new roof. We move in the fall (maybe it's spring?)—it's gloomy and cold and the days are short. The night we go to look at it for the first time it is raining. My mother says it's good to see a house in the rain, to see if the roof leaks, to get a sense of how it will feel. The roof didn't leak, but everything else did—the windows, the doors, the cellar.

I'll still go to the same elementary school, but on Brook Street I'd been a walker. Here, a bus stops a few houses down the hill from us and fills up with kids. I'll ride it once but don't like it—I don't know anyone. From then on I walk, even though my school is now a mile away. The most direct route is to cut across the saltmarsh, but no one cuts across the saltmarsh. To step into it is to enter into another medium. It is muddy and filled with broken things—pieces of houses, pieces of boats, broken fences. Boards with nails. Dead animals. Sinkholes. You have to be careful where you put your feet, you have to pay close attention.

Something about it, something familiar.

The smell of it, the taste.

Querencia—from the verb *querer*, "to desire"—describes a place where one feels safe, a place from which one's strength of character is born, a place where one feels at home.

It will take almost an hour for you to cross it, if you move quickly, but you don't move quickly. You dawdle, you get lost in whatever you find, you arrange things. You pretend you are in a desert, you pretend you are being chased. The grass draws shadows, the mud holds them, but the air is light. You rise up into it, you breathe it in, then you sink deeper into the shadows.

A car passes, far away, on the road into town. You wonder if it's your mother, on her way to work. She came to you when you cried out in the night, put her hand on your forehead.

Querencia.

The marsh will never catch fire. No one can ever surprise you here.

You will always see them coming.

pink room

IF YOU WERE HERE WITH ME, in the shadow of the willow outside our house on Third Cliff, I'd point up to the window of my mom's bedroom. When I was your age, I'd tell you, there was no upstairs, not at first, not until Travis came. Travis, the Vietnam vet, the second and last man my mother would marry. Like Vernon, he was a carpenter, and so, like Vernon, he would build a room for them—a bedroom, above and away from my brother and me, left to fend for ourselves in the drafty rooms below.

First there was nothing, then there was a room, with a bed that nearly filled it.

A little balcony, a sliding glass door.

The walls were painted pink and in the middle of the pink Travis painted a heart—crudely, with his big paintbrush. Within a year a redheaded woman would come to our door after midnight, naked and panicked. Her boyfriend, it seems, had thrown her out, when he found out that she'd been fooling around with Travis. My mother, I'm told (though I never woke up), wrapped a coat around her, gave her a glass of whiskey, and sent Travis off into the night with her, to deal with it. After that, Travis set up a cot near the bed, the bed he was no longer welcome in. Then he moved the cot to a house he was renovating, with plastic for windows, torn and blowing

in the wind. Then he was gone, and one by one his stuff followed. He'd let himself in when my mom was at work and I
was at school. I saw him once when I'd come home early, I hid
in a closet when I heard his truck on the gravel. I saw how he
moved through the house, how he moved through everything,
as if he were still on patrol. How he spoke to his broken tools,
to his bag of guns, to the dog, who lay on the floor, eyeing him.
How each object he grabbed seemed to ignite in his hand.

A photograph exists of my mother in this pink bedroom,
looking out from a pulled-back curtain at the willow where
I'm standing now, the pink walls like flames behind her eyes.
Even (especially?) to me she's nearly unrecognizable inside it—
inside that photograph, inside that room, inside that moment.
    In the photograph I can almost hear her thinking.

She thinks:
    Children are like fish, really—they move through rooms,
    bump into the glass, open their mouths, expect food to
    simply drop in.

She thinks:
    Like fish, you could watch them in the act of their forgetting,
    you could watch them as they forget.

She thinks:
    Always at my feet, always twirling or hiding or dropping
    their clothes in little piles.

She thinks:

I stopped bending down finally, I stopped waiting up, I stopped listening at night.

She thinks:

What if I just stood here, let them drift?

What you need to know is that in the years after the fire, after we left the house on Brook Street, after we moved to Third Cliff, for a few years at least, until Travis showed up, my mother was present, she was loving, she was fiercely protective. This is how I remember her. Then, after Travis left, something inside her broke. I think it's safe to say that she never really found a way to repair it.

as we drive slowly past
the burning house

WHENEVER A SIREN—POLICE CAR or fire truck or ambulance—would puncture my Saturday morning cartoons, twisting the blue from the sky, my mother would tell me to go start the car. *Let's see what's happening*, she'd say, and we'd drive, to the place where the sirens called us, to a family huddled in their pajamas on the lawn, just like we'd once huddled.

Think of this as our *Odyssey*.

Sirens called out to Odysseus as well, to lull him into stranding his ship on the shoals—it could be argued that our sirens were merely calling out to strand us as well, only it would take years to know that was what they were doing. Or it could be argued that at least it wasn't our tragedy, at least we were able to step outside our house for an hour, into the fresh air, to witness something outside ourselves. To empathize, or to practice empathy, even though we never knew the people who'd lived in the burning houses, nor did it seem we cared to, even after their house was gone. What could we have possibly offered—a room in our falling-down house? (*there was no room.*) A meal, a blanket, some clothes? (*we never did.*) What was my mother hoping to find, what was she hoping to see? Was she teaching me to pay close attention to the world, as it was, or to pay close attention to the afterworld, as it would be? Maybe she believed she could tell if it was a scam by looking everyone in the eye as they stumbled out of their smoky house. Or maybe she just wanted to make sure all the children made it out okay. Or maybe she wanted me to practice, like other families practiced fire drills, so that when the sirens came for her I'd know what to do. To get in the car and drive, toward the sound, whatever it was—fire or heart attack, car crash or suicide—to get out and stand on the sidewalk or on someone's lawn. Or to not even stop, to make it a slow drive-by, while the stranger is carried away on a stretcher. But where do you drive to when the siren is outside your own house? What do you look at when the strangers on the sidewalk are looking at you?

mrs. parent

MRS. PARENT SHOT HERSELF in the head one night. Her house was perched on the edge of the saltmarsh. At high tide the water touched her porch. The floorboards, during a storm, must have been nearly submerged, saltwater seeping into her dreams.

The night she died I went toward her house at dusk, called by the sirens. It was just across Kent Street, through some scraggly trees, off the far edge of my grandma's yard. I watched as her body was carried out on a stretcher, the stretcher covered with a white sheet, a blossom of red where her head should be.

That night my mother told me what happened—Mrs. Parent had made dinner for her two boys, and when they finished eating they stood up from the table without a thank-you. They were on their way out the door, leaving their dishes for her to clean up. She'd had enough of their thoughtlessness—she took out a gun, told them that she was tired of their rottenness, told them that she was going to kill herself. One of the sons said, *You wouldn't dare*. The other son said, *Go ahead*, and so she did. My mother told me this story as the ambulance was pulling away. I could still hear the sirens, I could still see the lights swirling around us as she spoke.

The trails of breadcrumbs my mother left for me are some-times like this—more apocryphal than offering any sort of usable map. I now remember that as an even younger child I had said the same thing to my mother, one snowy night, as I ran around the house naked, refusing to get dressed for bed. My mother had said she was going to throw me outside in the snow if I didn't do as she said. *You wouldn't dare*, I answered, the thrill of a strange new power surging through me. Then, surprisingly, she grabbed me, opened the door, and threw me out. I stood on the porch for a few seconds, trying to cover my nakedness, then ran and hid behind the stonewall in the neighbor's yard, the same yard I'd stand in a year or so later, watching the shadows of flames cross the face of our house.

antigone

MY MOTHER AND I are driving down a highway. I'm fifteen, it's the middle of the day, I don't know where we are going. My mother is in another hard place—Travis has just vanished. She's cut off all her hair, lost a lot of weight. I'm beside her, and though we have nowhere to be, she apparently misses our exit. As we pass it, she remembers, and cuts the wheel sharply, so sharply the whole car goes into a spin—once, twice—like slow-motion. I look at her as we spin, I never say a word. We end up stalled, nose pointing into the oncoming traffic. Cars sound like sirens as they swerve around us. She holds on to the wheel, I look at her. A man presses his face to his window—tomato-red, close enough to touch—laying on his horn as he sails past.

Death is but a moment that returns forever.

We sit for a long moment like that, listening to the horns, then I reach out and touch her shoulder. She half glances at me, reaches for the key, turns the ignition. The engine struggles, then catches. *Shitbox.* She puts it in gear, gives me a wild-eyed look, as if asking if we should just keep going, gun it into the oncoming traffic. I look back at her, calm, as if we have all the time in the world. A car passes close by my window, laying on the horn. *We're okay*, I say, and point toward the exit, as if it were just one of many options.

the daily ketch

MY MOTHER IS NOW A BARTENDER. The bar is the Daily Ketch. A ketch is a type of sailboat. In Boston there is a famous fish restaurant called the Daily Catch. The word Ketch is an attempt to play off that fame without getting sued. The homonym defense.

When I was younger she'd bring me to whatever dive she worked in.

The Ebb Tide. The Cock & Kettle. The Bell Buoy.

The smell of alcohol soaked deeply into each one.

Like my father, it oozes from their pores.

She'd set me up at a table, feed me chicken in a basket.

The Daily Ketch is on the edge of a beach town—Marshfield—nearer to the ocean than to the center of town. It is a place where workers go, you might call it a *dive*. The workers all know her from the bank, where she's a teller. Do they know she has kids? They stand around the pool table, they haunt the jukebox, they sit at the bar. If it's the day shift she'll prop the door open to the sun.

Bars like this have one function—oblivion. Once you make your way inside there are endless ways to disappear. One can stare into the tablets of the jukebox, finger hovering over the numbers, seeking the perfect song. One can be propped up on a pool cue for hours. My mother is wiping down the counters, a nearly continuous action, from when she comes in to when she leaves. There is always something to wipe up. We've moved into the other house, the house made of weather. No one will bother her here because this is a gangster bar, and her boyfriend—Liam—is a gangster. She's waiting for him to come in through that door, like the sun.

Each song the jukebox plays is a song the gangsters like to hear.

> *Elvis*
> *Sinatra*
> *Frankie Valli*
> "Louie Louie"
> "Low Rider"
> "Suspicious Minds"

Her hair hangs down, like when she was a teenager. In a couple years Liam will convince her to quit this second job. She will still work days at the bank—she can make more money by simply depositing the gangster's cash without asking any questions.

Laundering is the colloquial term for what she will end up doing.

My mother stands behind the bar, opening bottles, pouring shots, but she isn't really here.

She hasn't been here for a long, long time.

rusty nail

MY FRIENDS AND I RIDE our motorcycles over to the Daily Ketch one afternoon. We are old enough to drive but not yet old enough to drink. Inside, the drinkers are already lined up on the stools. Some turn when we walk in, some simply stare into their bottles. My mother looks up and smiles. At the far end of the pool table a guy is holding his hands over his pool cue as in prayer. Waiting for the shot to be made; you can see in his eyes he is about to lose.

My mother's back is to a mirror lined with bottles, but she is not reflected in it. I go up to the bar, pretend I'm a stranger. My mother plays along.

What'll it be? she asks.

Rolling Rock, I answer.

She shakes her head, puts a tumbler on the bar, pours a couple things in it, hands it to me. A glass filled with ice cubes that look like skulls.

Try this, she says.

What is it? I ask.

Rusty Nail, she answers.

My friends love my mother. She gives us all Rusty Nails, *on the house*. She takes a fistful of quarters from the cash register and spreads them out on the table before us. Play a few songs, she says. Shoot some pool. Enough quarters that the song will never end. Line quarters up along the edge of the pool table and play all night.

The ocean can be heard in the moments between songs, the moments between pool balls colliding.

The ocean is everywhere.

Soon Liam will walk through that door. He will pass her a tiny fold of paper to get her through the night. She will vanish into the bathroom for a couple minutes, the murmur of the bar lost beyond the door. I'll talk to Liam while she's gone. The door to the parking lot is still open, darkness now pushing inside. Cars go by, headlights like scythes. In a couple years, when it's clear I'm going nowhere, I'll get a job with Liam.

jukebox

IF SHE WERE STILL HERE, my mother might tell this story:

I am the girl at the jukebox arguing with a guy about the song I want to play. I do not want him to choose, but in the end he will choose. In the end he will end up being your father. This is what I never told you. The song I wanted to play was "Bye Bye Love" I shouldn't have been wearing a crop top, I shouldn't have been wearing those shorts. I knew him from the coffee shop, he came in to get coffee for his crew. He was digging ditches, it was summer, the days were long. I ended up at the jukebox, no one noticed I was gone. He said, Play whatever song you like. *That was all it took. I just wanted to choose the song. I just wanted to be somewhere else. He was somewhere else. He was still wearing his work clothes, he offered me a beer, even though I was too young. I forced it down, he drained his. I still had to finish high school, I would never finish high school. I needed to get out of my house, my house was collapsing. It would take years to get over that song. "Bye Bye Love." Two kids later, bouncing from couch to couch, where could I be? All I wanted was to be inside the song. All I wanted was to be inside the bottle he was draining. All I wanted was for him to swallow me.*

Or this:

Once I was the girl leaning against the jukebox, listening to the man who would become your father. I'm sorry, I didn't know it'd be you. Now whenever you smile I see his face, and I remember this moment, leaning on another jukebox, trying to choose a song. A few minutes from this moment to now, he will walk up beside me. Beauty, he will whisper, and I will listen. I knew what he wanted. I knew I was not beautiful, and now here I am, still in a bar, another jukebox—another pool table. And here comes my son, who appeared in the word beauty, *who stepped out of it, with that face like his father's face, a face I cannot even look at sometimes. One minute it's beautiful, the next minute I want to cut that smile out of his body.*

communion

I'M EIGHTEEN. MY FRIENDS AND I think of ourselves as outcast, misfits, but maybe we're just drunks. Two shadowy girls with the same first name end up hanging out with us— let's call them O and O. They show up at our parties with pills they've pilfered from their parents' medicine chests.

I'll end up with one of the Os, who will become my first love.

One Saturday night, I'm in my room with my O, making out. The other O is making out in my brother's room with my pal John. My brother is up at college. My mother is out, tending bar. At some point we come up for air, step out of the adjoining bedrooms, meet up in the kitchen to have another drink. O (not my O) wants to write something down. She finds a yellow legal pad, reads a few lines of what is written on it— suddenly sober, she hands it to me, tells me I should read it. It is a note in my mother's handwriting. The first line reads, *By the time you find this I will be dead*. O didn't have to read much to know what it was. Undated, I didn't know if my mother had attempted suicide after writing it, nor did I know why or how long it had been kicking around on that yellow notepad. I didn't even know where O had found it. I remember feeling that something essential about me—some dark secret, some shame—was now on the table. I made up a story on the spot. I told the two Os and John that it was likely written a few years earlier, when her second marriage, to Travis, had ended. She'd had a hard time then, I told them, but she'd come out of it. I made it up. I didn't know anything about anything. We were drinking Jack Daniel's. After reading it I took the note into the yard and doused it with Jack and burned it, all five pages of it. I held each page up by a corner until the flames took. I sent each of my mother's words back into the universe.

A few months after burning the note I convince my pal Doug that we should go to Europe. He has relatives in Belgium where we can stay. I find round-trip tickets for two hundred dollars. I'm still with O, and I'll miss her the whole month I'm in Europe. The night I come back, I call her. We go to Peggotty Beach, the dark ocean spread out before us. We pass a bottle of peppermint schnapps back and forth. She has something important to tell me—she's been to a doctor, she'd been diagnosed with a terminal illness. She only has two years, at most, to live. My head fills with bees. Don't tell anyone, she begs. She wants to die with dignity, she doesn't want anyone to treat her any differently.

I swear both my secrecy and my love.

A month later I crash my motorcycle, with O on the back, into a stonewall. We're both drunk. I break her wrist, rupture my spleen. We end up in the emergency room. I'm in the hospital for a week. I'd already decided I wouldn't go to college, that I needed to stay close to O, to my mother. I needed to keep them both alive. After recovering from the crash, I begin working for ServiceMaster, a cleaning company—a guy named Skip has a franchise in my hometown. Each morning I show up in a blue uniform, drive a yellow van to strangers' houses. We do carpets, windows, whatever. One of our main jobs is to show up after there'd been a fire. We'd be in those houses for weeks. I'd stand in the center of each room, set up my ladder, and start with the ceiling. Everything had to be touched with a chemical sponge. I'd unscrew each light bulb, wipe off the soot, a bucket of warm sudsy water beside me. At one job, a girl stops by, to get something from her bedroom. It's her house, she'd escaped the fire. We were there to bring it back, to make it home again. I show her the sponge, how I wipe it over the oily soot, how it leaves a bright white line. This is how it was, I tell her, this is how it will be. I don't tell her it will always smell of smoke, that the sponge cannot rid the house of that. Something burned, and now that something will always be something else.

A year later, I begin working for Liam, the gangster my mother is dating. O needs money for her doctors, the gangsters are mostly just smuggling marijuana, I'm perfectly fine with that. After working for them for a year, I'll start college. I'm deeply conflicted about leaving both O and my mother at home, but I'm beginning to go off the rails. Cleaning houses, working for gangsters, I drink. At college I drink more, but I'm also reading Shakespeare and Blake, and having tortured affairs. My girlfriend is dying back at home, I tell them, as a way to explain my leaving. I tell myself I am a creep for cheating on her, and a saint for being with her. I have endless reasons to get fucked up.

I read *Paradise Lost*. I read Dante's *Inferno*. In the *Inferno*, Dante is making his way out of hell, trying to get to Beatrice. In real life, Beatrice was a woman Dante barely knew, yet he projected an enormous amount of energy onto her—she became his muse. If the *Inferno* can be read as a metaphor for depression, then Beatrice represents salvation. In the *Inferno*, Dante and Virgil come to the end of their journey together, blocked from going farther by a wall of fire. Dante knows that Beatrice is on the other side of the wall, and that the only way to get to her is to go through the fire, which he does.

I didn't tell anyone about my mother and her note.

I had burned it, it was gone.

I ride my (new, bigger) motorcycle home most weekends to work. The gangsters now call me "college boy."

Five years after swearing my secrecy to my O on the beach, the other O takes me aside at a party. She tells me she knows I'm fucking around on O, and that she understands why I'm doing it. I get teary. I admit that I'm not handling the dying thing very well. O has been studying to be a nurse, for the same reason I'm working for gangsters and going to school—so we can help O.

O isn't sick, she tells me. She's been making it all up.

Fuck you, I respond, that's a horrible thing to say. If it was true then the entire way I'd structured my life up to that point would mean nothing. Yet her words sank down to somewhere deep inside me. A couple weeks later I break down with O. I say I'm just not handling it very well, her dying. We are in my bed. She stops, holds my head, looks deeply into my eyes.

Then why don't you just start believing I'm not going to die? she says.

I pull away. What do you mean? I ask.

I went to the doctor last week, she says. I'm in remission. I'm cured.

Why didn't you tell me last week? I ask. Why did you wait?
This is good news, she says. I thought you'd be happy.

I end it with O after that night, and go back to college that fall.
I still drink, but not as much. I feel like I'm landing on earth,
after drifting for so long in outer space. I feel focused. I settle
down with one of the women I'd been having an affair with.
In December that year my mother kills herself, and I end up
drifting through the next many years. If I found a woman who
was pure and honest, I'd lie to her. If I found a woman who was
cruel and manipulative, I'd ride it into the ground. I became the
boyfriend your parents warned you about. I managed to find
a few women whose mothers had killed themselves, which we
took as communion.

book three

each one wraps himself in what burns him

dark energy

THEY SAY YOU CAN ONLY KNOW what you are capable of knowing. They say that if you get caught in a black hole the laws of physics don't hold. They say that the universe is made up of 70 percent dark energy, 30 percent dark matter, that less than 1 percent is what we think of as *us*—what we can see, what we can measure, what we can understand. So much, almost everything, is unknown. Yet without dark matter there would be no mass, and without mass there would be no atoms, no stars, no planets, and certainly not a hundred children making a whirlpool out of a summer day.

Some nights, after my mother got home from waitressing, as she was undressing for bed, she'd point to me, then point to her stretch marks, those tiny purple snakes crawling up her belly from somewhere far below. *You did this to me,* she'd say. I knew what she was saying, I knew it was true. *Annihilation.* I had ruined her body by being inside her body.

This body. Her body. I have carried it so far.

James Joyce offers this:

> *The radiance . . . is . . . the whatness of a thing. This supreme quality is felt by the artist when the esthetic image is first conceived in his imagination. The mind*

> *in that mysterious instant Shelley likened beautifully*
> *to a fading coal . . .*

A fading coal. Let's call every word my mother uttered *dark matter*—light bends around it in spooky ways. Some days it seems I could hold it in my hands, everything she said. Some days this is all I know of radiance.

When our child is two years old, I begin an affair. My wife and I had gotten married just a few months earlier. I made vows but (clearly) I didn't believe them. Some days the only tangible thing between us was our child. If asked I'd say marriage is an invention of man, but a child is an invention of God. I would like to believe that before the affair began, in the days and weeks leading up to it, I tried to let my wife know I was struggling, that the distance between us was becoming so vast I worried we would soon be unable to traverse it.

I met S at a friend's place in Boston. She was in town for a few days, sleeping on his couch. I noticed she was reading Robert Duncan, I asked what she thought of it. I showed her my favorite poem of his and I read it out loud to her, the title bleeding into the first line:

> *Often I am permitted to return to a meadow*
> *as if it were a scene made-up by the mind,*
> *that is not mine, but is a made place . . .*

It's a poem, in part, about the power of the imagination, about how we return, again and again, to the source of our dreams, to our childhood landscapes. The next morning we all had breakfast at a local greasy spoon, and it turned out S and I were both going to be at a writing conference in a few months in Portland. I told her I was planning to go a couple days early, before everything started, to spend a few days on the coast. I asked if she'd ever seen the Oregon coast. I said she should go early as well, that we could meet up, explore.

If she needed to, I said, she could crash with me.

listenerland

AT TWELVE, THIRTEEN, I fall asleep to the radio's soft murmur. It puts someone else in the room with me. It makes me feel less alone. *Ladies and gentlemen, let's give Mister Al Green a hand.* A star (satellite?) crawls past my window. *He's asking for help, ladies and gentlemen,* his eyes turned upward because *up* is his idea of heaven. Apollo's up there—stranded, failed, twenty-two thousand miles from home—only a roll of duct tape can save them. Upstate, a guard lies dead in Attica and no one knows what will happen next. Al Green falls to his knees, a prisoner drops to the ground, my eyes close. Everything falls into something else and I try to hold on to the falling. *Ladies, gentlemen, look up*—our astronauts are still there, surrounded by suns, their radio dead and the nothing is getting closer.

Now here I am, years later—married, a child, no longer alone—yet the radio is still on, murmuring softly in the next room. Marriage, the idea of it, not to mention its reality, never hung loosely on my shoulders—it felt, rather, like a weight pushing on my lungs, slowly crushing me. I showed up for it, but some part of me I kept hidden, safe.

I remember finding that board in the woods behind my grandmother's, just off the path to Mr. Mann's. How I lifted it, and underneath I found those six baby mice, blind and squirmy. How I didn't know where the mother was. How I slowly lowered the board back down over them. That's what marriage was to me—it was the board and it was the blindness and it was the abandoned mice and it was the way I never told anyone about any of it.

Here's how it felt, in the midst of the struggle:

> *You wake up next to your wife at three in the morning and you can't breathe. The demon inside murmurs that you will always be unloved, that you will always be alone, that isolation is the safest place to be. This voice, which sounds a lot like your own, a lot like your mother's, has led you to many dark places. You take off your wedding ring because it feels like a noose around your neck, even though you know it is just your finger. You know it can't strangle you, yet that's how it feels. You don't want to think about it, but when you say you can't breathe maybe it's simply that you never found your way out of that burning house.*

In *The Trauma of Everyday Life*, Mark Epstein offers this:

> *The mind's primary defense against agony is dissociation and . . . the primary motivation for dissociation is stability. . . . In dissociation the personality wards off becoming fragmented. It does this by withdrawing from that which it cannot bear. The shocked self is sacrificed, sent to its room for an endless time-out.*

My wife, like each of us, has her own demons. Both she and I are on the road a lot for work, but not together, not usually.

We both spend a lot of time in motels. Maybe, for each of us, these motel rooms are simply an endless time-out, a safe place for a few hours, a few days. Each room is contained, we just need to find our way out of it. Part of us knows they will kill us, these rooms. Part of us wants to die in them.

Janis Joplin snarls, *It's all the same fucken day, man.*

It is very likely that I am only speaking for myself here.

Yet I married a woman to whom it seemed I was utterly replaceable, which at first suited me fine, but eventually made me feel like I was little more than a ghost, passing through rooms that would never be mine. The fact that I haven't figured my way out of that burning house was—is—a central sadness in my marriage. At some point along the way I had convinced myself that my wife simply left me back there, alone, that she never offered a lifeline out. When I said I was lonely in my marriage, when I said I couldn't breathe, this was why. I do not blame her. *You go on, I'll catch up later,* has always been my mantra. The radio murmurs its dull arithmetic: *This is going out to all of you out there . . .*

amber

ALL THE YEARS ON PEGGOTTY BEACH I'd never noticed that the stones there are so colorful. I touch one to my tongue—the spot I make is almost psychedelic. The day my daughter gathered them I was humbled that I'd never taken that in, amazed that she could see them as precious. If I hadn't been sleepwalking through my boyhood, or if I'd dropped acid sooner, maybe I'd have been able to see that as well. Maybe I'd have known that one day my mother would walk barefoot over those same stones, that it'd be a day in December, the day she'd die. I might have wondered if she'd jump from stone to stone on her way to the water. I might have wondered if she'd be able to feel them below her feet—how round they are, how perfect. I might have wondered if that would have changed anything.

When I was my daughter's age, America was a place of cults and witches, black magic and the paranormal. A man on tv could bend a spoon with his mind. Strangers slid in through open windows at night to rearrange your furniture. We woke up to pentagrams painted on cemetery walls. I was in my bedroom, attempting astral projection—my body is here, seemingly asleep, but my consciousness is far, far away.

The promise was this: *one could be forever elsewhere.*

When I am her age, I tack a photograph to my wall. In it, a boy and a girl stand at the edge of the ocean. The boy is younger than the girl—they are holding each other's hands, as if they were about to waltz. I study it like a talisman.

The younger one, afraid of the waves.

The older one, attempting to calm him.

The thing was, I knew they could be me, both of them, both the one afraid and the one calming the one afraid.

My hometown was on the Atlantic Ocean. It gets trashed every winter—still—in the eventual storms. All the houses along the shore washed away. I didn't need to read books about hurricanes, because they were everywhere.

Alma. Ella. Celia.

We heard their names on the radio.

Driving up the coast in their swirly black Cadillacs.

Here we go again.

Years later I will fall in love—let's call her A. I'd quit drinking a couple years earlier, I was coming out of my dream. It will turn out that both our mother's had died the same way, we must have sensed it the moment we met. One night I told A the story about the storm that destroyed my hometown—it didn't have a name. When the storm hit, O and I had just gotten together—maybe I should have taken it as a sign. Part of me believed that if I told A about it, that if I then brought her there, to my hometown, to the edge of the Atlantic, it would make her love me, or at least understand.

But she never did *(come to my hometown? understand? love me?).*

One night I told her that I didn't believe in ghosts, because no one ever came back, no matter how much I prayed. How I would have given anything just to see my mother once more. Yet, after it ended between us, she did come back (A, not my mother). But it wasn't really her, not how I remembered her. I'd been waiting for her, but we were both damaged essentially and in the same way, which made it hard to see, like when two mirrors are lined up across from each other, how the tunnel of it bends.

Years later, I was lying in a field. I couldn't remember how I got there. I would tell you that prayer was all I had left, but I don't think that's true. That was the year I kept finding myself on my back, looking into the sky. Everything I had tried up to that moment had come to this: alone in a field looking into the sky. I might have named it God, because (like the ocean) it was bigger than me, and didn't care.

If one could be forever elsewhere, why was I still here?

I'd reach out my hand into the endless blue, but it kept moving farther from me.

Today I read that scientists can reconstruct an object by photographing its shadow. What this means is they can go into a darkened room, project a dim image onto a screen . . . a computer reads the flickering shadow, and in a few minutes, voilà, a blurry image of a toad.

Or a tree.

Or the lost beloved.

I remember my mother, watching that unnamed storm on tv. How she covered my eyes whenever they showed a body floating past. How I saw them anyway. Maybe that was how I learned to pray. After it had passed, I went down to the ocean, the ocean I had listened to all night. I could taste it on my lips.

The storm had passed, I found things it had left behind—in the breakwater, in the marsh. I lay on my back—everything gets washed away. The woman I loved is with someone else, the children in the photograph let go of each other. What does it mean? I stood on the edge of the ocean, I wanted to pull myself beneath the waves. I bought a mask, flippers. It is quiet down here, calm. I am holding my breath now, I am reading my favorite book. My mother is holding on to my wrists, just like her wrists were held when she was little. I am not afraid. I am full of salt.

haystack

IN THE MONTHS BEFORE PORTLAND I tried to make things work with my marriage—we read self-help books (*Getting the Love You Want*; *Mating in Captivity*), we filled out forms, we made dates. Maybe if I'd told her that I was going to meet up with someone when I was in Portland, that part of me wasn't sure what might happen . . . but that's not what I did. I could claim that part of me didn't believe that anything would happen, but part of me wanted something to happen.

A few months later I land in Portland, rent a car, drive to the coast. The motel looks out at a rock formation called Haystack, rising like a medieval city out of the shallow water at the edge of the beach. I get there a few hours before S does. The motel offers a room with a king-sized bed, but we don't really know each other, not that well, so I take a room with two small beds. I remember waiting on the beach for her. I remember that enormous rock, covered in seabirds. I remember her walking toward me across the sand. I remember the little tidal pool she had to navigate around. I could see what was coming, like storm clouds pushing over the ocean.

That night nothing (everything) happened—by nothing I mean we slept in our separate beds. By everything I mean it was clear we were at the beginning of something. At any point in the night one of us could have reached a hand out across the darkness that separated us, but neither of us did, not then. At that moment what we were sharing could fall into the category of *a small intimacy*—it wasn't something I told my wife about.

I wrote a poem after that first night together—it wasn't innocent, but, I told myself, no poem is, really. I didn't show it to S, not right away—it was charged, and at that point I could still tell myself that it was simply a feeling, inside me, nothing more.

After Portland, S and I went back to our lives. But we began checking in, at first once a week or so, but then almost daily, her voice in my ear as I bicycled into the city. We lived fifteen hundred miles apart, and so it was safe, I told myself, to talk. Years later she'd tell me that I'd told her, at some point in those first months after Portland, that I was lonely—it still doesn't sound like something I'd admit to, even if it was true. I was recently married, had a two-year-old child. I found it all to be thrilling. And tiring. And weird.

And, yes, lonely.

Filming was to start in a few months on a memoir I'd written. I'd be on the set while Julianne Moore would reenact my mother's suicide. On the day of the reenactment I call S.

I get to meet my mom today, I tell her.

Dark, she says.

Where else would I be? I answer.

How are you holding up? she asks.

Everything is moving very quickly. Even the director wonders what I'm doing there.

Go home, he says. *You don't have to be here, not today.*

No, no, I say, *let's do this.*

What I don't say is that I'm unsure what he means by the word *home*. That I haven't felt it, maybe since my mother died, likely for years before that even. Maybe since the fire, which, in some ways, was never extinguished. In the days after watching Julianne—her ocean, her pills, her gun—I'll turn to S for comfort.

We'd been in ever-increasing contact for almost a year by this point, and had even slept together once (a few months after Haystack), yet we now became lovers.

whose dream is this?

I AM ASKED TO WRITE something for a friend's (Jim Peters) retrospective. I base it on one of his photocollages (*Studio with Black Painting & Reclining Figure*, 2011), which he made with his partner, Kathleen Carr. In it she is lying face down and naked on a bed in their studio.

Here is how I began:

> You've been inside this room, you've felt this before. She will, some part of her, always be turning away from you, some part will always be leaving. Some part of her will never be yours—maybe no part of her, maybe none of her, ever was. *Not yet once more please please again.* Here in this room the TV is never on, the bed is never made, no one ever wears clothes, not here, not together. What is this? Another annunciation? The moment before the angel, sent down to tell you how your life is now forever changed, touches your shoulder? If so, then hold onto that moment, the before— paint it, write it—because once the angel finds you, once she whispers the word into you, it will be impossible to turn back. *Back* is the ground you once stood upon, *back* is each bent blade of grass (*the beautiful uncut hair of boys*) pushing into your back from the

dirt below. Your hand reaches up to her—in a room, in an echo, in an opening—and the walls push in. Outside the window it is night, outside the night is, well, that's like asking what's on the far side of the moon, like asking what's beyond the bend in the universe. You cannot imagine it. You cannot *not* imagine it.

As I wrote it became a mirror, in some ways, of my life with S, as it was unfolding. Every week I was traveling back and forth to Houston, where she was based. Our days in Houston began to take on a feel of domestic, if fraught, bliss.

The end is a small gasp, as if surfacing, as if you've been underwater, as if you haven't been breathing. Then the shudder, then the twitch, then your body is no longer yours. Your body fills with electricity then, then you are no longer in control, then a voice not your own comes out, unintelligible—*too much, too much*—an animal sound, wounded, dying—a dying animal.

Then it whispers inside that no one can touch you. Then the small cry, then the cough.

On cue, she laughs at the cough. She always laughs at the cough. You wonder out loud if the cough is because of the fire. She thinks you mean the fire you'd just created with your bodies, but what you mean is the smoke you had to run through, almost fifty years ago, the smoke that you're just now thinking is what makes you feel like you cannot breathe as you lay beside her at three a.m. What you meant to say is that when you made it out of that burning house you never expected to find someone there beside you. What you meant to say is that you never expected—nor did you want—anyone to stay.

We could say this is just a moment, just a room, just two lovers, people fuck (or not) behind every window, it's just what we do. Yet each of them, each of us, contains the universe, which is just beyond these walls. Of course your lover's ass contains it, the bend in the universe and the whatever unnamable beyond. Our bodies mirror the curve of the earth seen from thirty-five thousand miles, just as this wall contains all the hands that manifest the wall, just as the parade of lovers coming before and to come. . . . If you can say, *Touch yourself while you look at me*, if you can say, *I want to see you make yourself come*, if you can let her hold your wrist while you jerk off, resisting for a moment falling into each other, allowing her to see you, for once. . . . We want to see ourselves, to be seen, at that moment of adoration, of annihilation, we want this moment to stretch into forever, we want it to press out from these walls, these sheets, that clock. Of course we can make this moment contain everything, yet none of this matters, it is only a threshold into something larger than ourselves. Than flesh. We set up the tripod, we hang the mirror, we glance at ourselves, sometimes we catch ourselves glancing, into our own eyes. We look into ourselves as if into a stranger, uncomprehending, as if the answer were there, in these stranger's eyes. Is this who I've been all along? Is this the me outside of who I am?

bright thread

ONE STORY I HEARD when I was first sober was that if, as a drunk, you were a good horse thief, then you'd be a better horse thief sober. I took this as one of the promises of sobriety—I was unable (unwilling) to see it as a warning. It was, for me, by and large, true, if by *horse thief* you mean *liar*. But, a year or so into the affair, I'd come to a place where I no longer wanted to be that person—call it a type of spiritual bankruptcy. I'd begun to catch glimmers of what it might be like to actually land on this earth—but it wasn't immediately clear how one puts down the reins.

Months would pass without seeing each other. I'd try to be in my marriage and S would try to get on with her life. I could tell myself the affair was over, that it had been something sweet I'd always remember . . . then two more years passed, held together by the bright thread of her voice. I became the man in the playground, the cord of his earbuds clenched in his teeth (think *bit in a horse's mouth*). So the mic is closer to his voice, so his lover can hear him above the endless screams. Instead of a horse thief, I'd become the horse. I told myself that the damage, if there was any, was contained. I told myself that it was perhaps the only thing that held my marriage together (part of me still believes that). I told myself that I felt no shame about it (that has changed). I told myself that it took the pressure off, I told myself I wasn't hurting anyone, I told myself that it was simply what a horse thief did. I told myself that everything was as it should be. My daughter (my daughter!) was swinging behind me, wild on the monkey bars. In a week I would travel to California and my lover would meet me there. I had become the father in the playground having an affair, and nothing (*nothing?*) about it seemed wrong. My lover heard my daughter grow up—*two, three, four*—and she will even end up watching her, when it turns out I have no child care in California. They will build sandcastles and collect seashells while I work. That night my daughter will give me a drawing, all of us—*mom, lover, daughter, me*—one big happy family.

When asked what he would take if his home were on fire, Jean Cocteau answered, *I'd take the fire.* Did he mean he'd save his house, or did he mean he'd carry the fire with him from then on?

After five years, I finally check back into therapy.

My wife, seeing I was struggling, had gotten a referral from her therapist.

She passed me a folded piece of paper with a name penciled on it.

Dr. Mee, in our first session, tells me I have the ethics of a drowning man.

Drowning in flame, I think.

~ ~ ~

centralia

CENTRALIA IS A TOWN WITH ROADS but (almost) no houses, trees but (almost) no people. No big box stores on the outskirts, no downtown. A coal-mining town with no functioning coal mine. Recently, the U.S. postal service discontinued its zip code. A drive through the Pennsylvania mountains to Centralia is like a drive into nothing—*tree, tree, broken stonewall, trash.*

Centralia has been on fire since 1962, or maybe since 1932, depending on which story you believe. The fire is underground, following a vein of anthracite through the mining tunnels the people who once lived there built. *Anthracite* is another word for coal. Some geologists say it will burn for two hundred and fifty more years. No one knows for sure how it started. One story is that the volunteer firemen set the dump on fire, as they did every year, only this time they left some corner of it smoldering. Another story is that a trash hauler dumped hot ash into the mouth of an abandoned mine, then drove off. It's that kind of place, at least now, the kind of place where someone might feel okay unloading a truckful of trash in a field. I don't know what it was like in 1962, but on the drive over now you will pass many such homemade dumps. A refrigerator, a washing machine, a stove, knocked over and rusting in the middle of the woods. In 1962, of course, there were houses, and people—it was, after all, a town. Now it is no more a town.

You can drive down a boulevard lined with driveways branching off it, but now they lead only into trees. Some roads are blocked off; if you walk down one of these roads the asphalt might split open beneath your feet and a rope of thick white steam might seep out. It is still possible you would step wrong and fall into the hot center of the earth.

This hidden fire has slowly eaten away the town. Nearly all the houses are gone—in each the refrigerator exploded, in each the windows were smashed with an ax, in each the carpet was made of petroleum—poof. In one story, from before everything was gone, a man goes into his yard, completely brown now, puts his hand on the dead grass, heated to one hundred and seventy degrees, and falls headfirst into the hole his hand has just made. One church is still standing, along with three graveyards—depending on your beliefs, you might find this fact strange, or telling. Seven houses are also still standing—the owners are allowed to stay in them until they die, or until they burst into flame, whichever comes first.

The last time S and I will be alone in a hotel room it will be in a town in the Pennsylvania hills, just downwind of Three Mile Island. We tell ourselves we are trying to know whether we're really broken up this time, or whether we should move forward. But forward into what? A white picket fence? Some sort of polyamorous arrangement? We'd already come so far together, we still had some shared hope for a future, but would that be enough? At some point we will take a break to drive to Centralia, which we discover, when we look at a map, is only an hour away. I carry within me the story of my house catching fire, and here is a town where every house caught fire.

the book of splendor

FLORIDA. I'M TREADING WATER, over my head, floating (*dead man's float*) in the warm, warm Gulf. My daughter is swimming in the motel pool, just past those dunes. I can't see her from where I am, nor can I hear her, but I know she's there. She's being watched over by a writer friend. When I come back she will have a gash on her nose and a nasty sunburn.

Not doing so well, I find myself saying, to the salt, to the sky.

When my daughter was born—once she'd healed from the trauma of birth, once she'd been cleaned of meconium and blood—her skin was flawless. As in, *not a mark on her*. This went on for three years. At the end of this flawless period, this period of seeming perfection, I briefly wanted to keep her that way forever. *Unmarked. Unhurt. Unscarred*. Yet, almost as I heard myself articulate it, I swear the next day, *bammo*, she fell and split open her cheek, just below her left eye. I had to butterfly it together to keep her from vanishing.

That morning, in our Floridian motel room, my daughter hit me with a stick. Just me and my daughter this time—no girl-friend, no wife. All morning my daughter had been swing-ing that stick too close to my head. I'd asked her more than once to knock it off. The stick finally connected with my hand, so I pulled it from her—maybe too quickly, maybe too aggressively—and snapped it in two.

She curled up on the motel bed and cried.

I sat in the chair, listening.

I want mama, she cried, over and over.

I want mama, I want mama . . .

Well, mama ain't here, I answered.

Her mama was away, working. I held my head in my hands. I am not someone who snaps at his daughter, at least that's not how I see myself. Now I was the one doing the crying. She sat up, came over to me, put a hand on my head.

It's okay, Daddy, she said. *It's okay.*

I'm trying, I say, *I'm really trying.*

I know, Daddy, she says. *You're a good daddy.*

We landed in Florida the night before. In the supermarket, on the way to the motel, I stood before the chips—so many choices. My mantra was, *Hold it together, hold it together, hold it together.* Now, over my head in the warm, warm Gulf, my mantra is, *Please help me*, but I'm unsure who it is I'm talking to.

A tern hangs in the air above me.

Will I come back from this? I wonder.

Have you ever actually been here? comes the answer.

On the plane from Brooklyn I'd been reading the Kabbalah. In the beginning were only two books: *The Book of Creation* and *The Book of Splendor.* One was about what we could see, the other was about what we could feel. One was about a god who could be known, the other was about a god who would be forever unknowable. It was the second century, and this was enough.

A wave breaks in my face.

That night, in our motel room, my daughter and I watch a movie about an astronaut stranded on Mars. He spends his time making little videos of himself, which he transmits back to the rest of us stranded here on Earth. At one point, when it seems he will be saved, he tells himself, or us, or God, *I'm really looking forward to not dying.* And then his potatoes died.

That's all I remember of the entire movie.

The next morning I woke up and remembered that life simply goes on and on, even without us. The next moment I wondered if it hadn't already stopped. It is possible that, just before I fell asleep, I prayed. If I had, it would have been for my daughter, or happiness, or both. Or maybe I thought I should but no words came. I don't know what to ask for, I said, to no one. Everything, it seemed, was ending—my marriage, my job, my home. Yet nothing ever ended—my childhood, the fire, bewilderment.

On the radio in our motel room, a theoretical astrophysicist—Carlo Rovelli—was talking about time. He said: *A stone is a thing because I can ask where the stone is tomorrow, while a happening is something limited in space and time. A kiss is not a thing, because I cannot ask, where is a kiss tomorrow?* I thought of the stones lined up on my desk: a stone is a page in *The Book of Creation*, while a kiss is a page in *The Book of Splendor*. Then I think: What is the difference between a god who is knowable and a god who makes himself known? Then I remember that prayer: *Days pass and the years vanish and we walk sightless among miracles.* I woke up this morning and thanked no one, my dreams dissolved in my mouth like salt in the ocean. I'm treading water, the air is overheated. This morning my daughter hit me with a stick. We are from a place formed by ice, I told her, as I broke her stick over my knee. *Lord, fill our eyes with seeing and our minds with knowing.* Later I'll be facedown on the sand. My hands will form a small bed beneath my face. I'll close my eyes and see the glacier coming. A doctor held my head when I was born, my mother kissed the top of it, still wet with her. *The Book of Creation* has been with us all along, while *The Book of Splendor* was begun just yesterday—each day we are offered a chance to add to it. Does this mean there is a god somewhere whose medium is words, and by those words he created all that surrounds us? I can understand a world made of words, I do it all the time. I'm doing it now. I am not floating in the Gulf of Mexico, I am not asking for help. Where is this world made of nothing but splendor? *Help us to see, wherever we gaze, that the bush burns, unconsumed.*

find me when you wake up

I come in late. I miss the beginning.

On the bright screen Tom Cruise dangles from the ceiling of what appears to be a military transport plane, wearing some sort of metal robot suit. Other soldiers dangle in their metal suits on either side of him, as if they are hanging from clothes hangers, as if they are no more than gowns in a closet.

Bombs explode all around them. The plane is being fired upon, but I don't know by whom. In the metal suit his arm can be a gun, but Tom doesn't know how to turn off the safety, so he will not be able to kill anything, nor will he be able to defend himself. He yells for help, he yells that he doesn't know how to work his suit. The other soldiers shake their heads. One jokes that Tom is already dead—*I see a dead man in those boots.*

Inside and outside it is very loud.

Then the plane is hit and many of the other soldiers are sucked out through the hole now blown into the fuselage, but not Tom. Those soldiers are now dead, we imagine, even the one who joked that Tom was already dead. A sergeant yells for Tom to hit the red button that will release his body from the plane, but Tom is afraid—like me, he doesn't know what's happening.

As the plane collapses around him he finally hits the red

button—his body drops into the nothing and dangles from a wire beneath the damaged warplane, swinging wildly through the air in his heavy metal suit, as other bodies in their suits swing and dangle wildly around him.

I find this all unspeakably beautiful.

~

I spent the previous weekend with S on the Oregon coast. We had agreed to meet again at Haystack, the site of our first (innocent) weekend, only this time to break up. We sit side by side on the sand, facing the distant rocks painted white by the shit of seabirds. It is as eerie as I'd remembered. We haven't seen each other in six months. I tell her the story of the years after my mother's death, of living on potato chips and cottage cheese from mini-marts, perhaps as a way to justify my failings.

When my mother died I was in the midst of my addiction— her death turned up the flame beneath it. Every moment that followed—the phonecall, the cleanup, the funeral—all of it, I was wasted. I was the one who cleaned up her blood (it pooled perfectly round), because there was no one else, because it was all that was left, because I wanted to touch her once more. I used a bowl and a rag, I watched as her blood swirled down the drain and away. The year that followed I never went inside—I would pull up to our house, the house she'd died in, and simply fall asleep in the car. The morning sun would wake me, the car sideways in the driveway. I slept on friends' floors, in friends' beds. I slept with all my friends, but I couldn't sleep, not really. I stayed awake, wasted, for years—feral, animal (S and I used to find that word in our mouths when we made love—*animal*, we'd murmur to each other—*animal*). I decided to set up my life as a series of rooms I could drag myself to, of doors I could close, and inside each I placed someone who could hold me.

~

Tom drops to the beach below with the rest, into the middle of an awful battle—*a Normandy, a Somme, an Antietam*— where a huge crablike robot will kill him, where crablike robots will kill everyone. But before, or as, the robot kills him something happens to Tom that will cause or allow or force him to relive the same day, to do the same things, over and over. As soon as he dies the day begins again—*reset*, this is the word they use. No one knows how or why the day will keep being reset but we have to simply accept it as fact in order to continue to watch the movie, which is itself continually being reset.

Tom is killed by the jellyfish robot, then cut to Tom asleep on a duffel bag in the middle of a military base—no beach, no robots, no explosions. Was it all a dream? Tom is kicked awake by a drill sergeant, ordered to stand, to get ready for battle. Tom tries to explain that something strange is happening. He tries to explain that he is not combat-ready. *Look at me*, Tom says, *do I look ready?* Tom is about the same age as I am, and no, he does not look ready. The sergeant—the same sergeant from the plane—knew he was going to say that, it is written on a piece of paper in his pocket.

The soldier will say he is not ready.

~

In *The Believer*, Laurie Anderson offers this:

> ANDERSON: ... in *The Tibetan Book of the Dead*, for
> forty-nine days [after you die] you're in the Bardo, and
> it describes in a really fascinating way how you lose
> your senses and how your mind dissolves as you pre-
> pare for another cycle. At the end of that forty-nine-
> day period, you are born in another form ... I wanted
> to study that particular Bardo, and then I found that
> that's only one of the many Bardos.

For more than forty-nine days each sunrise would find me
asleep, sideways in my car, but maybe I was, yes, simply passing through, bardo after bardo.

~

Early on, Tom meets a woman on the beach—he has only
repeated this day once or twice at this point, not the thou-
sands he will end up repeating it. This woman is fierce—a
warrior—much fiercer than Tom, by far the best fighter the
humans have, way beyond battle-ready. In their first encounter, as the robots spiral wildly around them, tunneling inexorably through the sand, he manages to let her know, with a
word, that he has done this before. By finding her, by naming
it, by her being able to hear him, she sees him, if only for
a moment. Just before he's killed once again, she tells him,
Find me when you wake up.

~

> ANDERSON: ... the great thing about the sky is that
> it's available, twenty-four hours, to everybody, unless

you're in jail, and then you have to go to your mental sky, which is there as much as the physical one, so you can have that. If I'm confused, I just spend some time looking at the sky and, you know, falling into it. It's not a meditation that anyone taught me, it's something I've done my whole life, and liked doing, and it made me feel like nothing. I enjoy that feeling. That's what I go for—not to be here.

BELIEVER: Did it make you feel like nothing or everything—or is that the same thing?

ANDERSON: Same thing. It was a fabulous feeling— of lightness and happiness. There are things in your childhood where you have to say what your name is and pretend you're a person, but I'm still not really a person, and I never really had to be a person in that way, because I feel like this other way of understanding the world makes more sense to me.

Watching the way his body moves, I don't know if Tom Cruise feels like he's pretending to be a person, if he feels like his name is not who he is, but it seems that way. I've always thought that he inhabits his body as if he didn't quite fit into his skin.

I get it, that feeling.

The film is called *The Edge of Tomorrow*, but I call it *The Edge of Tom*. It will be considered a box-office flop. Yet, even though I doubt it's true, I think it's a masterpiece.

~

In *The Body Keeps the Score*, Van der Kolk points out that when trauma survivors watch violent movies, their bodies release as much opiates as someone being prepped for major surgery.

The violence, in this very specific way, calms them.

Not only is there a high body count in *The Edge of Tom*, but the same people get killed over and over again—mangled, blown apart, punctured—each time in a slightly different way.

Tom returns to the same handful of scenes, over and over, which seems close to my experience of trauma. Freud called it the "compulsion to repeat"—we repeat the trauma so we can gain the illusion of mastery over it. Over and over I watch the scene where Tom overcomes his fear and hits the red button that will drop his metal-suited body into the sky to dangle from the end of a wire beneath his ruined warplane.

The joke that Tom is already dead will be repeated many times in the next two hours. The beach will always be on fire.

~

At Haystack, I told S that I was tired of being a horse thief, that I wanted to be a better person, but I wasn't sure I was ready. We'd been seeing each other off and on for four years. When we were apart I'd try to mend things with my wife, to see if we could make something of our marriage. But, like Tom, I kept finding myself back on the beach. Like Tom, I kept fucking up the ending, which gave me the chance to get it right. At this moment, this means letting S know how much she has meant to me, which lets her see how much I am suffering at saying goodbye, which lets her forgive me.

Could it be that simple, that I just want to be forgiven?

But forgiven for what?

~

ANDERSON: The other Bardo that is happening is the Bardo that we're in right now—in which we both believe we're having a conversation in a studio by the river when, in fact, we're not.

BELIEVER: What are we doing?

ANDERSON: Well, I think illusion is one of the most interesting things that I've found to think about. I don't really know how it works, but I know that in some way we are and in some way we're not having this conversation. Just look at yesterday, and what you were doing, and how important it was, and how nonexistent it is now! How dreamlike it is! Same thing with tomorrow. So where are we living?

It will take Tom a long time, an entire movie, to find his way off the beach.

~

When S and I first met we were both sober, but for several months she's been out. Now she's trying to get back in—failing, trying, failing, trying—like many of us who struggle do. Going out is simply what we do—the miracle is each day we don't. But I knew that much, or at least some, of our shakiness came from what we were doing, our affair, which meant we were actively cultivating a secret life. Sobriety, they say ("they" being folks smarter than us), demands *rigorous honesty*. Yet it seemed we couldn't figure out how to simultaneously be together and be honest.

We were, those years, yes, legislating as we wished.

When we agreed to meet at Haystack it was with very low expectations. Yet I wanted her to know, whatever happened, how grateful I was that it had been her I'd been with on this journey. Whatever happened next, our love had delivered us both from one hard place to this (hopefully) better one. But her months out had left us both weary, wary, stunned—they echoed, somewhere buried deep inside me, my experience with my mother, and her struggles. When S and I had first met, she was the same age my mother had been when she'd set our house on fire—maybe some part of me wanted to understand that recklessness. The past several months, with many early morning phone-calls of the *incomprehensible demoralization* variety, had begun to bring our recklessness to the surface. S had twenty days sober when she stepped off the plane, yet we couldn't know then if, through an act of grace, it would last.

~

Here's Tom again, dangling above the beach in his iron suit.

> **BELIEVER:** Do you have thoughts about death and what happens after death?
>
> **ANDERSON:** Well, no single person who has ever lived will be able to tell you what happens. Period. Nobody's right and nobody's wrong. So what do you do, then? With my experience, and how my mind works, and what I think about—let's call it "the disappearing mind stream"—when you follow your thoughts and watch them attach to certain things, it makes certain

things real and other things unreal, and you realize that this is all created by your mind.

Here's what I believe: *You can survive anything if you believe that one person in the world is wild about you.* Or this: You know how a child will prefer a swimming pool to the ocean? Maybe our motel rooms were like that—safe, not only because we got to make the rules when we locked the door behind us, but because inside those rooms we were contained, like children in a swimming pool, rather than over our heads in the actual ocean.

~

Parker Palmer, the theologian, when talking about his own struggles with depression, offers this:

> As I worked my way through that darkness I some-
> times became aware that way back there in the
> woods somewhere was this sort of primitive piece
> of animal life. I mean, just some kind of existential
> reality, some kind of core of being, of my own being,
> I don't know, maybe of the life force generally, and
> that was somehow holding out the hope of life to me.
> And so I now see the soul as that wild creature way
> back there in the woods that knows how to survive
> in very hard places, knows how to survive in places
> where the intellect doesn't, where the feelings don't,
> and where the will cannot.

Haystack in the distance, thick with seabirds. The woods Palmer is talking about are metaphorical. His depression allowed him access to what he describes as a "primitive wildness" inside him. Waking up in my car was my woods. The affair was my woods. We'd been trying to break up since May, but the thread between us, made mostly of words, was still there. *I miss your voice*, one of us would text the other, and off we'd go.

Bright thread, I called her.

~

On the beach below—bloodbath, setup, slaughter—the battle rages on. In one version Tom saves the fat happy soldier, in another he lets the fiery wreckage of the warplane crush the fat happy soldier.

After a thousand or so lifetimes Tom learns that he cannot save everyone.

The ship has been hit, the bodies dangle from the underside, swinging wildly. If two bodies collide they both die. That one guy keeps saying the same thing—*I see a dead man in those boots*. Each time Tom comes back to life (*one day at a time, keep coming back*) it looks like the same day, but he learns that he has to break the pattern. In the addict's world doing the same thing over and over leads to death, or at least to being trapped inside a very small life. In Tom's world doing the same thing over and over leads to perfection—he learns, by the end, how to kill the robots, which, since this is a summer blockbuster, is all he really has to do. In the end he simply has to save the world.

He learns to hit the red button to drop his body at exactly the right time.

He learns how to make it across the beach.

He makes it off the beach.

centralia

AN AFFAIR TAKES PLACE IN DARKNESS, in shadows. My lies had allowed the affair to go on, but for a year or so they'd begun to have a corrosive effect—my life was getting smaller and smaller. I don't generally think about my soul, but there it was. I thought about Centralia, about the houses that weren't there, the fires we could not see. I thought about that hotel, just downwind of Three Mile Island. I liked being in a hotel room again, I liked being able to close the door—some part of me might never not like that.

We left a light on, I wanted to see her.

She left her contacts in, so she could see me.

A week earlier S had confessed that she had another lover. It wasn't the infidelity (is that even a word that can be applied to this situation?), it was that for the past year we'd been actively trying to practice honesty with each other as a way to move out of the affair. I'd felt no shame, until that moment, and suddenly there I was—wading, falling, tumbling, spiraling through shame. A trapdoor opened beneath my feet. As Winnicott notes, *Babies who are not adequately held have the fear of falling forever.* It was a strange sensation, to suddenly know deeply a feeling I'd only ever known from a distance. Or else I knew it so well, and for so long, that it was the air I breathed. They say a fish is unaware of the water it lives in, and maybe I'd been swimming in shame my whole life. It woke me, and all at once, and as I woke I felt, for the first time, how fucked it was that I was even having an affair, how fucked it was that I was spreading damage—hurting my wife, my lover, my daughter. Who else was I hurting? I asked S if she would wait for me when I came out on the other side of this, but I had no idea what that would look like. Then, a few days later, like a veil dropping to the earth, I saw how fucked it was that my mother had set our house on fire with me asleep upstairs. I felt unloved suddenly and from all directions at once. Unloved— what I'd spent my life not allowing myself to feel, confusing the word *love* with the word *run*.

erasure

THE FIRST TIME I CAME HOME after sleeping with S, I swear (*out, damned spot*) my infant daughter knew. I couldn't hug her, couldn't look her in the eye. *I'm home*, I yelled, then went straight into the shower. That was when I still believed it could be washed off. Five years later I came out, only now she could speak.

I know where you've been, her eyes said.

I know who you've been with.

For those years, I spent so much time burning up my immediate past—erasing texts, deleting phonecalls. Erasure—this is what an affair is, what it becomes. I write this on a scrap of paper, as a storm rains down:

It's like you keep forgetting who I am.

It's like I'm being erased.

The affair is grinding to its end. Weeks go by without any contact. She is trying to move on. I am trying to be honest.

When I write the word *erased* something tugs on my subconscious, like an echo. It reminds me of something buried deep inside me, something I have no desire to look at. If my mother thought of me, asleep upstairs, could she have lit that first match? Ten years later, if she thought of me in that moment, would she have been able to leave? The fact is, we are so lost inside ourselves sometimes that it is impossible to think of other people, even those we love.

On the radio an expert is talking about lying. Everybody lies, this expert says, every day. I have been telling a lie for years, about how well my mother loved me, how that love allowed me to thrive. It hit me, a few weeks ago, that this was both true and not true. It came as I was trying to drag the affair into the light. To either stay in my marriage or be with S. The story of an affair, I would come to learn, is different when the husband doesn't understand how much he loves his wife. For many years I told myself that the affair held my marriage together, and this too was both true and not true. A bright red thread connected me to that lie. Red as blood. I told myself that my mother loved me even after she set our house on fire, her love a tiny red flame in each of her eyes. I had to run through those eyes to escape.

Only later would I understand that a bright red thread stretched from the flames in her eyes to the bullet in her heart, red to red.

doctor mee

I SPENT LAST NIGHT IN THERAPY, talking (again) about home. How I haven't felt it, maybe since my mother died. About my wariness now at the idea of creating a home with anyone. When we try to change, my therapist pointed out, often our old behaviors come roaring back to reclaim their place in our lives. One of my old behaviors, or the thing that has steered me to this place (and allowed me to survive), has been to do anything to deny that feeling of being unloved. As a child I wouldn't have survived if I saw clearly the complexity of my mother's love, and so I created the story that she loved me well, and that it was her love that got me through. Forrest Gander offers this: *Creepy always to want to pin words on "the emotional experience."* Affect is precisely what the stories I've been telling myself have allowed me not to feel— by containing this emotional resonance in a story I had an illusion of control. If I can tell the story in such a way that I find my way out of the burning house it will prove I have some control over the chaos. If I can break into Mr. Mann's house then I can master the terror I now feel in my own house. I always said I made it through my childhood because I felt loved, which is both true and complicated. Maybe it is more accurate to say that the story I created, my *cover story*, kept me from feeling unloved.

Maybe my mother set the fire to find that sense of control as well.

the ultra-living

IMAGINE WALKING DOWN A MOTEL hallway, each num-
bered door painted red, the numbers either going up or going
down. Someone has just stepped out of a shower, someone has
cracked the window. The tv is off. Sometimes you have to keep
doing the same thing, again and again, even if you couldn't,
if asked, explain why. Maybe you'd say, *I am wired this way*,
maybe you'd say, *This is the way the world works*, maybe
you'd say nothing, maybe all of it is true. In Centralia, one day
a fire reached up and touched its first house. Then, just before
Christmas, my wife's job ended and she came home. She saw
I was in some sort of crisis, she asked if I was having an affair.
I had come to the end of lying, which I'd been so good at for
so long.

  This was the ultra-living moment.

  It lives in our hearts, it lives in the sky.

  I answered *yes*.

  It was Christmas Eve.

innocence

I told her.

Everything?

Pretty much.

So not everything.

She didn't want to know everything. Not the details.

What happened?

She just asked.

Why would she ask?

She asked before, but I always denied it.

You didn't deny it this time.

I said yes.

That makes no sense.

It was a yes-or-no question. I said yes.

Maybe that's progress.

I hesitated.

You must have come to the end of it.

I couldn't find the other word.

No?

I used to be so good at it.

Lying?

More like not saying everything.

Specious is a subset of *lying.*

No one can know anyone completely.

She hardly knows you at all.

Now she does.

Pretty picture.

But I told the truth.

Now what she knows about you is that you've been lying this whole time.

I'm not sure where I am.

I can imagine.

Before I only had to not say a few things. Now I'm supposed to say everything.

photograph of a boy when he imagined the future as fire

HERE'S A PHOTOGRAPH OF ME as a boy, a few months before the fire. I'm sitting in a chair beside a table, my feet don't quite touch the floor. I'm not wearing shoes. The sun falls on the right side of my body, pushing me farther into the shadows. My right hand is fully in the sun, each finger illuminated, almost as if on fire. The chair has legs, the table has legs, I have legs— I will need these legs, soon enough, to run. The room I am in is seemingly made only of boards, the boards are unfinished hemlock, simply nailed to a frame to become *wall, floor, ceiling.* More boards make the furniture, these boards are lightly sanded, only slightly more finished than the walls. The boy in this photograph does not look out at the camera, at whoever is holding it. No one else is in the room with him, except for the faces someone has taped to the walls, which make a type of wallpaper. The faces are torn from magazine or posters, some are full-sized cutouts: a woman holds a baby before her as if it were an offering; Santa offers a bottle of Coca-Cola; a dog, tongue out, looks happy just to be alive; a ghost-woman (the one face the boy almost never looks at) looks directly at him, as if she could help. The boy never looks into the camera, or into the sun, or anywhere, really.

the end of the afffair

I had come to the end of lying, so when my wife asked if I was having an affair, I answered, Yes. When put this way, it might sound as if I put no more thought into it than taking off a glove, which isn't true, not even close. Gradually, a chasm had been widening below me—a chasm between me and my story, between me and my family, between me and the universe. I'd been practicing jumping over it all my life, yet only recently could I see it was full of rats. The affair was, perhaps, simply the latest manifestation of that chasm. There is the me on one side, and the me on the other, and as the space between the me and the me widens, I begin to lose sight of myself—one becoming unrecognizable to the other. On one side I am standing with my daughter's hand in mine, on the other side I am standing with my lover's hand in mine. I look over the edge, I'm on the top floor of a hotel, the chasm of Miami spread out below. It is all window, that room, brightly lit and cavernous. I touch the glass and it moves, it shivers. I could break it with a word, with a thought. Beyond the window I can see the ocean, rain falling into it, the top of my building in the clouds. All I can imagine is a few days alone, silent, empty. A few days blameless.

mister mann

Tell the story of Mr. Mann, my daughter pleads. It is a few months before I will reveal the affair to my wife. We are driving back to my hometown, the town that contains all my stories. I want to show her Mr. Mann's house, I want to walk his fields with her. I want to hold her up, look in the window I fell through. My daughter is seven, she carries a stuffed monkey with her everywhere—his name is Monkey. She speaks to Monkey, Monkey answers. My wife—her mother—is away again, working out of town for the next several months. She'll come home when she can, but for now she is nowhere in sight. My daughter and I are solo, and as the weeks pass we will go feral—showers are no longer required, she can wear whatever crazy thing she wants. As we pull into town I begin to doubt, seeing how small she is, that I could have been seven when I broke into a house guarded by a man with a shotgun. I must have been twelve, I decide—it's something a twelve-year-old might do.

Today, this is the story I tell her:

> *The winter after I broke into his house, Mr. Mann died, froze to death in his bed, after his heat was shut off for not paying his bill. When they went in to clear out the house, to figure out what to do with it, someone found a loose floorboard, and beneath*

it they found a small metal chest. As incredible as it sounds, in the chest they found a million dollars' worth of Spanish doubloons. There is, of course, a story connected to that: As a seven-year-old, Percy Mann (like me) liked to wander. Sometimes he'd wander all the way to Third Cliff. His family farm included a piece of the cliff—farmland, in those days, often included a sliver of waterfront. It was dusk. As he lay on his belly looking out at the water, he saw a ship at anchor—a pirate ship. Hiding in the brush, he watched a pirate row ashore. He watched as this pirate hauled a small metal box inland and buried it beneath a tree. Percy watched the pirate row back to the ship, then he went to the tree and dug the chest up. Inside, he found it full of doubloons. He dragged the chest home and hid it beneath his floorboards. All those years later, whether he knew he was living on a small fortune, or whether he had forgotten about it, we cannot know. Those who found the treasure used it to make his home into a museum. The Mann Farmhouse & Museum. The house was built in 1636, the museum opened in 1976, eight years after Mr. Mann died. I'd never gone inside it, not since I broke in, uncomfortable with the fact that we used his money to make a museum, after letting him freeze to death.

When we pull into Scituate, we learn that the museum is closed for the season. We'd come so far. I knock on the door, a woman answers. She's familiar, in the sense that we'd both grown up drinking the same water. I explain that I knew

Mr. Mann when I was a child, and she offers to open the house for us. This is how I enter Mr. Mann's house for the second time in fifty years, this time not through a window, this time holding the hand of my seven-year-old daughter.

Percy Mann, it turns out, was a collector of many things—toy railroads, sailing equipment, farm tools. His collections are now laid out—dusted, organized, labeled—which is not how I remember his house at all. Nowhere do we see any small cardboard boxes holding scrolls of serialized stories from the newspaper, stitched together with thick black thread. Upstairs, we see the spot in the floor where they found the doubloons—one floorboard pulled aside, plexiglass over a small chest, imitation coins spilling out of it. I ask my daughter, out of earshot of the caretaker, if we should donate our scroll, once (if) we find it.

No, my daughter hisses.

songline

I'D KNOWN THE STORY of my mother setting our house on fire for twenty years. As I stood outside Mr. Mann's, holding my child's hand, the story began to dissolve, into pure *affect*. I began to ask what compelled me, every day the summer I was seven, to follow that path through the woods to a man my grandma said would kill me. How had this become the safest place for me to be? Then I began to wonder about my mother, about her dissociation, about how lost she must have felt, to find herself alone with two kids when she was barely twenty years old. She always told me she'd never really had a childhood, she always said I should enjoy mine while I could. It always seemed she'd fled hers as if it were a house on fire.

Epstein (again) offers this:

> The shock of trauma sits outside awareness like a coiled spring. The emotions aroused—which by their very "unbearable" nature cannot be imagined— are left unexplored. The self that moves forward is restricted by its failure to integrate the traumatic impact, by its failure to process its unbearable feelings. In its attempts to "ensure that what has already happened is unlikely ever to be repeated in the same way," the defense of dissociation splits the self into a fiefdom of incompatible states.

I can't say why it feels so important visit Mr. Mann's house with my daughter, except to show her one of my fiefdoms. For the next two years, each May my daughter and I will make this drive back to my hometown. On the way she will ask me the name of my fourth-grade teacher, but I cannot tell her. Just as I cannot tell her the names of my classmates. Or what the room looked like, or what we did in it. What I can offer is the story of Mr. Mann, of the treefort I built with wood from his barn, of the saltmarsh I crossed every morning on my way to school, of the house we lived in across from the fire station, the one I stood outside of in my pajamas, watching as it burned. What I can do, all I've figured out to do, is bring her to each of these stations of the cross. On these trips we always end up, at some point, back at Peggotty Beach, the beach that protects the salt-marsh from the ocean. I used to walk this beach, the morning after the Fourth of July, looking for firecrackers, unexploded. I could smell them, the gunpowder. And the salt, which pushed against the glacier, the salt that pushed it back. I could hear it at night as I lay in my bed, I could hear the stones being ground smaller and smaller by the waves. How even each grain of sand was being ground smaller. I could hear the waves themselves— building, breaking. I knew the water would one day gather itself together and pull me—all of us—under. Every winter it happened, the nor'easters came, named for the direction they came from, which was, of course, the direction the glacier came from, all those years ago. My little town, little more than a sandcastle pulled together by a child, with her plastic bucket and her plastic shovel, washed away each winter. It might take eons, but does that make it any less tenuous?

zero gravity

THIS IS WHAT I LEARN: flame only resembles liquid because of gravity—that's what makes it seem to flow upward. Like us, it is always trying to rise. In space (zero gravity), a flame, if it could breath, would be a sphere. You could hold it, in your awkward gloved hands.

This is what I will learn: that I don't know what to do with desire, where to put it. I sometimes wish I existed in zero gravity so this desire, this flame, would be a sphere, something I could hold, instead of always jumping out of my hands.

What is the opposite of fire?

My mother lights her matches one by one in her car, her face illuminated briefly by each flame. Her face is there, then it is swallowed again by darkness. It is like a concert of fire, with the orange tip of her cigarette dancing each word. The car now a snowglobe, filled with smoke. Here is the edge of it, here is the window cracked. This is an archive of each cigarette your mother ever smoked, you even hope she had one last one before before before . . .

The word *fire* came to me in a dream, like a hand lifting my head. It sounded like my mother, it sounded like love. What is the shape of this love, then? Is it shaped like smoke, something that could slip out a cracked window? Is it the sound of quarters dropping one by one into a coffee can? Is it the way everything melts in the face of it?

Why did my mother never talk about the fire? Did she think she could get away with it, that nobody would ever know? One neighbor, her window overlooked our back deck. She could have seen my mother that night, hunched over her flame. The summer after the renovation the son of this woman shot my mother with a BB gun as she hung out laundry on the line. The BB stuck under the skin on her arm, a little blue bubble.

Just a dumb kid. *An accident.*

But I can't help wondering—did the son know?

Did everyone know?

Now I can see what it is to be seven, how the words of the story are the story, how they must come out in the right order. *Tell me the story of Mr. Mann.* But, just like my mother, I don't tell my daughter much about the fire, even if it was the fire that led me straight to Mr. Mann.

On the way home from our last trip to Scituate, she cried out from the backseat, *You had so many adventures when you were my age. You got to get your own dinner . . .*

photograph of the boy when he imagined the future as fire

HERE'S ANOTHER PHOTOGRAPH, in this one the boy is not alone—he's in the same house but in a different room now. The boy sits with his back to a wall, the wallpaper behind his head peels off in sheets—*sheets*, a word we use for rain. It's as if his back were the only thing holding up the wall, his halo in tatters. The wall behind him is a ruin, and if he doesn't move, if he allows it to seep into him, it will ruin his new shirt. His feet still don't reach the floor, the flashbulb burned into the forever of his eyes.

We can see through the doorway behind him into another room. His mother stands in the center of this room in a pile of her own undoing—it looks like ash has been swept up around her feet, it looks like she is either rising up from it or sinking back into it. She cannot see the boy, and he cannot see her. It isn't as if he's hiding, just hidden. Somehow the sun has gotten caught in the mother's hair, so it seems a cloud, or a light bulb. The mother wears a dress, it bells around her knees, just enough to let her ash fall out—it's as if she's already been cremated, as if she cannot hide the fire within.

~ ~ ~

sleeping beauty

THIS TALE, LIKE MANY TALES, centers on a kiss. Like many tales, it begins with an orphan, wandering alone in a forest. *Once upon a time, an orphan lived with his grandmother on the edge of a great wood.* As far back as he could remember, his grandmother had been telling this story, the story of the sleeping princess:

> *Deep in the forest is a tower, and deep inside this tower is a princess. Her jealous stepmother had cast a spell over her, a spell that put her to sleep for a hundred years. This tower is as large as a castle, with many chambers inside. Any child who discovers this tower will find the door unlocked, and when he or she goes inside they will become enchanted by the sleeping princess. How beautiful she is, how always she seems just about to wake. Only the kiss of the beloved can wake her, that's what they learn from fairy tales. Each child, of course, believes that it is their kiss that is the key, the one that will bring her back to this world—but when they try, they too fall into a trance. When they come out of this trance— a hundred years later—they find they've grown old, while the princess has remained asleep, and young. Being old, these now-aged children are always cold,*

always needing to build a fire. You can see them sometimes, wandering the edges of forests, bundles of twigs tied to their backs.

As she ended the story, his grandmother would point to the line of trees that surrounded them. *Can you see them?* she'd ask, but the orphan never did. Each day he would enter these woods—to gather wood for their fire, nettles for their soup—but mostly to look for his mother, who had wandered off into that same forest one day long ago. Tell me about my mother, the orphan would ask, but the grandmother would never tell him that story. All he knew was that she'd walked into the forest one day to gather sorrel, a day like any other, and never returned. All he knew was that she'd vanished. The orphan often believed he glimpsed her, in the distance, moving between the trees. Sometimes he told himself that she was the princess in his grandmother's story, that a spell had been cast over her, that she was the one in that tower, that she was waiting, all this time, for him to find her, to wake her.

~

A request appears in my in-box this morning:

In less than 500 words, can you describe a kiss? Or the kiss? That is, of all the kisses that you've experienced in your own lifetime, either as one of the kissers or as a witness to someone you care or cared about as they kissed, can you describe the kiss? And can you tell us what made it special, memorable, bright in the vault of memory? The kiss can be awkward or beautiful or unexpected or ugly or tender or cruel or sweet or . . .

nick flynn

In all of human history, what was it about this partic-
ular kiss, for you, that makes it unforgettable?

The kiss that came to mind is the last kiss I gave my mother—it rises up unbidden. It's dusk, she's upstairs, lying in her bed, coming out of—or going into—another migraine. It's just after Thanksgiving, I've come home for a few days for the holiday. I'm living outside of the house by now, finishing up my junior year at college. My mother is still young—forty-two—still beautiful, still desired. Young enough to start over. Her boyfriend (the gangster) has been in jail for a couple years now (he got caught smuggling drugs). He's up for parole in a month, but she's been seeing someone else. I've been out with friends, likely getting high in our cars, likely in the Peggotty Beach parking lot—these days I'm always high. I'm home now to say goodbye, to let her know I'm about to get on my motorcycle and push on, ride back up to school. I climb the stairs to her bedroom, the lights are off, a tiny orange bottle of white pills within reach. Her eyes are closed, her blanket is red, her skin alabaster—maybe she's a little high or a little hungover herself. The queen is in pain, maybe mortal pain, if she doesn't open her eyes she might never open them. The prince knows this, he's been wandering this forest his whole life, the bread-crumbs eaten long ago. The prince leans over her face, as he had done so many times, to whisper the words that will keep her there, only the words don't come, or they come out wrong. *Can I get you anything?* or *See you soon.* The voice that comes out of him doesn't sound like him. *Kiss her,* it murmurs, and so he does. Her eyes open, and the spell, for that brief moment, is broken.

eros & psyche

THE WAY THE MYTH OF Eros and Psyche unfolds, they can only be together if Psyche agrees to never lay eyes on Eros. They marry, move to a mountaintop mansion, yet they can only meet up at night, in darkness. Somehow, for years, they make it work. They make love without ever seeing each other.

In a very real sense, Psyche does not know Eros at all.

I grew up surrounded by many people I could not trust. Damaged, beautiful people. I learned how to survive within those parameters. Years later, like most of us, I was drawn to those who were familiar—those with whom I'd need to remain somewhat guarded. Those who were possibly even a threat, if I let my guard down.

So I never let my guard down.

This, unfortunately, was also true for my marriage.

~

At some point, Psyche's curiosity—or fear—overtakes her. She needs to know if Eros is a monster. One night, oil lamp in one hand, knife in the other, Psyche approaches Eros as he sleeps. She is prepared to kill what she loves before it kills her. When she sees Eros's face she is overcome by his beauty—*to be looking upon the face of a god.* In shock, she spills some hot oil on him. Scarred, he wakes and flees. She has broken their trust.

What can we take from this myth?

That a lot is better left unsaid, unasked?

What did my mother mean when she'd warn, *Get ready?* When she'd warn, *I won't be around forever?* As a child, to even ask such questions was to risk being cast into the unknown. Peel up the edges and you are in the realm of disaster. Look and turn to salt.

This can happen if you hold a lamp up to anything.

I cannot say there was any relief in the truth being revealed— after I told my wife I'd been having an affair, the days that followed, which became weeks, then months, were painful. Yet some part of the revealed truth made whatever had been murky and unsteady (which had allowed denial to flourish) more solid.

~

After Eros fled, Psyche spent her days searching for him. In desperation, she turned to Aphrodite for help, who gave her four impossible tasks. The final task sends her to the underworld, to retrieve a box which she's forbidden to open. Once again, curiosity overcomes her—she opens the box. Out pops Morpheus, who sends her into a deep sleep.

I woke up one day as if I too had been in a deep sleep. I looked around—I was married, we had a child. The ultra-living moment. Until then I'd been both the beast and the sleeper. I'd been making love in the dark, where no one could see me. I knew that part of me was hideous. I feared it was the part that held desire. Some part of me felt I'd been tricked into this life. That (like Sleeping Beauty) I'd woken up in a world I hadn't chosen. Yet no one had tricked me. I'd made the choice myself, even if half asleep. That other possible lives were flittering around me, like fireflies—this is true for everyone, isn't it? By choosing one I had to forsake all others (this is the part that I am only beginning to understand). Where had our passion escaped to? Was it simply air seeping out of a balloon? I'd been asleep so long. Would I stay? Or would I set up an alternate life?

Was it an illusion that passion could heal me?

Was it an illusion that love could revive me?

~

QUESTION:

After the revelation, did my wife want to know more?

Slowly. Not all at once.

QUESTION:

Did she want to separate?

Some days yes. I kept a go-bag ready, I bought a used Volvo (I thought of it as my *getaway car*). The underlife had dragged itself into the light, trust had been broken.

QUESTION:

Was she committed to staying in the marriage and figuring it out?

Some days yes, some days no. We'd been skimming along the surface, now the truth was on the table. This was four years ago now. After three years of couples therapy she wants to go deeper or say goodbye. I take this as an invitation, that some part of the broken trust is healing. I want to go deeper.

As these questions swirled around us, a fire in California destroys a community called Paradise. The fire was predicted, everyone knew that one day it would come. Yet, even knowing this, where, in the years leading up to the moment fire touched them, could the people of Paradise have gone? Could they have fled to another town, where it was certain that no tragedy, no natural disaster, would ever strike? Where is that town?

I sat in an empty apartment one day, in the weeks after the revelation, deciding if I was going to move. It was the apartment a friend had grown up in—vacant now—she had offered me the key. I felt a chill sitting there, a premonition that something bad was going to happen in that room, either to me or to whomever came to me there. I didn't feel at home in my marriage—it felt tenuous—but inside this empty apartment I felt something even darker.

I returned the key to its little lock box.

I went home.

home home home home home home home home home

home home home home home home home home home

beatrice

IT'S NIGHT, YOUR WIFE IS in bed beside you, checking something on her computer. Time passes. The world in her computer is vast, full of unspeakable damage—children missing, children abducted, children tortured. It seems this could go on forever. The steam from her shower rises off her body. You would like to make love, but the world on her computer is not making her think of that. It is, in fact, making her think the opposite of that—what is the opposite of making love? You're reading a book called *The Trauma of Everyday Life*, your wife passed it to you when she saw how much you were struggling. To be honest, *The Trauma of Everyday Life* isn't making you feel much like fucking either.

One passage rises up to say hi:

> *The Buddha did not always know that the world was on fire. Nor did he always have a feel for its bliss . . .*

In the days leading up to the revelation, as I rode my bike in the city, my eye would catch on a discarded bit of red paper, crumpled on the sidewalk, tumbling along in the wind. It would stop me in my tracks. I'd stare at it, hypnotized. This would happen several times a day. A red plastic grocery sack would fill with wind as I passed, rise up, menace. When I look it up in my dictionary of symbols, I find that red is both a life force (blood) and annihilation (fire). Creation and destruction. Robert Johnson sold his soul to the devil at the crossroads, singing, *The red light was my mind*. My daughter spills a cup of cranberry juice on the couch and I snap, a little too loudly, *You have to be more careful*. When I see the shock on her face I collapse in tears. I am falling apart. Everywhere you look these days you are looking into fire. Everywhere you look these days there is bliss. The world is on fire with it. It reminds you of Rilke: *After the new fear comes a new bliss. It has always been that way.* Then it is dark. At one point, before the affair, you begged your wife to leave the lights on so you could see each other, but that didn't work, not for long, not for her—like everyone, she has her own vanishings. You had to learn to make love in the dark, yet there was a problem—wrapped in darkness, she could be anyone.

By the end, she always was.

Dante, in his autobiographical *La Vita Nuova*, describes falling into a dream after an encounter with Beatrice on the street. Beatrice had said hello to him, and this thrills Dante so much that he names her *The Lady of the Salutation*. In the dream, which he describes as a "marvelous vision," Dante encounters the Lord, whom he describes as entering in "a mist the colour of fire." The Lord is carrying a sleeping Beatrice in his arms, who is "covered only with a crimson cloth." In one hand, the Lord holds Dante's own heart, in flames. In the dream, the Lord makes Beatrice eat Dante's flaming heart. This vision, thick as it is with red, is the beginning of Dante's descent into the Inferno.

Do you wish to rise? Augustine asks. *Begin by descending.*

Now things are better, you tell yourself, between you and your wife, now that you are on the other side. Now you are trying to find your way back to each other. Now, sometimes, if you're up for it, your hands find each other, or some part of each other, in the dark. Yet, when you do, sometimes still it's as if your hands are crawling over each other like spiders. Sometimes she'll brush your hand away, as if afraid it will bite her. Sometimes you jump a little at her touch, as if her fingers were full of electricity. Sometimes she puts your hand on her stomach, which is a signal for you to come out. *Come out, come out, wherever you are.* Sometimes now you are able to meet in the darkness and remember who the other is.

annihilation

A KEY FEATURE OF ANTIMATTER is that when a particle of it makes contact with its ordinary-matter counterpart both are instantly transformed into other particles, in a process known as *annihilation*.

Look again at that boy asleep in his bedroom. Night is all around him, it holds him. This boy, every cell in his body, has a counterpart, an *anti-cell*. Can we call what sleeps beside this boy, then, an *anti-boy*? Does the glass in his window, now framing the dark, have an *anti-window*? And his mother, wide awake downstairs, is she at this moment the mother, or is she the *anti-mother*? And later tonight, as the smoke rises up the stairs, as it enters the room of the boy, what will happen? Will his waking be slow, or will it be not at all? Will the smoke close his eyes, will it make the dark thicker? Here is the boy, about to wake up, here is the anti-boy, his hand on the door. When they meet they will both be instantly transformed, and we will call it, yes, *annihilation*. And when the anti-mother tries to stop the mother from climbing the stairs, through the now-thicker smoke, to wake him, will both of them also, yes, *annihilate*?

Yet, in daylight, she will, once again, be his mother.

Intact, he will only smell of smoke, but he won't be smoke itself.

~

On the radio, a man is speaking on the importance of repentance:

> *We cannot literally go back in time and undo what we did. And yet, repentance is precisely that process by which we can—in the moral realm, if not in the physical realm—we can go back to the deed, we can find that part of ourselves that led to doing the transgression, and reform ourselves. I find that inspiring, to think that we are not in bondage to even our most grievous mistakes.*

What did you want, the police to come the next day and take you from her?

Ocean Vuong offers this:

> *The most beautiful part*
> *of your body is wherever*
> *your mother's shadow falls.*

a jar of water

IN THIS JAR YOU SIT on the bank of a brook, you see the water for what it is, made of a thousand suns. You could have sat there forever, you could have died on that bank (clearly, part of you has). In the death dream you swear it was enough that your life had been full, happy, instead of waking up at three a.m. unable to remember where you are or who is beside you. Instead of waking up unable to breathe (*hello, married life*). You've been dreaming about a river, about a stick, about a boy who knew he was loved, a boy who kept pulling the stick in and out of the water, who knew what he could do and couldn't do with everything. It was so simple, yet why can't you breathe? You might as well simply write about the stick, if that is all you have, or the brook, as you press your stick into it, as you watch the water find its way around it, almost at once. *Everyday life is a trauma*, the Buddha proclaimed. *It is as if everything is burning . . .*

Yet here I am. Whole. Holy. When I tell my daughter about the fire she looks at the sun. I won't tell her that my mother— her grandmother—set it, just as when she asks how she died, I won't tell her about the gun. I'll say, simply, *She had a bad heart*—this is the only jar I'll offer. If you are reading this now, I'm sorry I lied to you—you were only seven, I didn't want you to know, before you had even fully landed on this planet, that your grandmother had chosen to leave it. I didn't want you to know that it was an option, that it was something in our blood. I didn't want you to know that at one point, when I was your age, she might have considered, with one match, to simply fold me—us, everything—back into the universe. Just as I didn't want you to know, at that moment, that I too had considered leaving.

kintsugi

MY DAUGHTER LEARNS HOW my mother died by seeing the title of one of my poems—"On the Anniversary of My Mother's Suicide My Daughter & I Take the A Train to the Museum of Natural History." I hadn't meant for her to see it. For some reason I burst into tears when she asks if it's true—maybe from grief, maybe from relief. I knew that one day I'd tell her, I just didn't expect it to be today. It's better, I need to keep reminding myself, to be living in the truth. This is why, for the past three years, each week I bring Dr. Mee my dreams. In one, I hug a boy who is the age I was the summer our house caught fire. He is my son, but he is limp in my arms. I tell him I love him, but we both know it's a lie. Later, I see him in a motel room, under crumpled bedsheets, which are covered in blood. The sheets rustle slightly, but I do not move toward him. I do nothing to help him, nothing at all. In another, more recent dream, a broken piece of pottery, blue and gold, sits on my desk. My initials are on it, from the year I got sober (the first time). It reminds Dr. Mee of *kintsugi*, the Japanese method of repairing broken pottery by using gold to bind the pieces together. In this way, the break becomes what is beautiful, what is valued. It is a way to embrace the flaw, the imperfect. In place of the break there is now a vein of gold.

Yesterday, I offered one of the stones my daughter had carried from Peggotty Beach to a woman who had lived through a fire. Her house had caught fire when she was a child—she had escaped, but not unharmed. We were in a writing workshop together (I was writing this). I had brought one of the stones with me, to remind me what I wanted to write about. Back home the rest are still on my desk—so heavy, pushing down on the air. I cannot say why they are still there, taking up so much space, except that they mean something. I wonder if my mother, as she carried her body to the edge of the ocean, as she crossed into it, could see how these stones contain both time and the slow erasure of time. How each is fifteen green bottles with nothing inside. I asked the woman who had lived through fire what I should do with this one stone. Her eyes were radiant, like fading coals. Scars rose up her neck like flames. The fire had not taken her words. I showed her a picture of my daughter, told her the story of how she had filled the trunk of my car with stones. One day my daughter will likely get a tattoo, I told her, or a piercing, or a real scar, one that doesn't go away, one that she will carry for the rest of her days. I told this woman that if I prayed I would ask for my daughter—for all of us—to be protected—not from all harm, but from the aftereffects of that harm. A month earlier I'd sat in a church at a 12-step meeting and read this: *They took my daddy in and they made him better.* It was a story about a child telling someone who was struggling that there was a place to get help, a sanctuary. It hit me deeply, at that moment. What it meant, I imagined, was that I needed to find a place for that boy who felt safest in the woods, in the saltmarsh, a place with enough room for all the wildness inside him. So he wouldn't have to leave part of himself back there in those woods, in that marsh. The woman who had lived through fire smiled, held the stone like a child in her lap, offered to take care of it for me, until I was better.

augury

LAST NIGHT MY DAUGHTER (now ten) looked around our apartment. *Something is wrong*, she said, *this doesn't feel like home*. I looked around. The white table was where it always is, the large photograph of the dead laundromat still hung over the couch. *What do you mean?* I asked, but by then she was on to something else, something to do with the dog, who seemed both interested and not. The dog's water bowl was empty. My daughter carried it to the sink and filled it, then spilled some on her way back.

I watched the spill expand, transform.

I read recently about a scientist (though he is likely more of a poet than a scientist) who believes that water expresses itself in a vast variety of ways. This scientist holds handmade signs up to the ocean, one word written on each—GRATITUDE; STUPID— an experiment. This is what he claims to have observed—the crystals in the water react differently to each word. Some move faster (STUPID), some move slower (GRATITUDE). Some move closer to the light (LOVE), some move away from the light (HATE). Afterwards, he looks at a sample of the water under a microscope—the crystals in water exposed to GRATITUDE, he claims, appear to be *more beautiful*.

What this scientist is proposing might have once been in the realm of the paranormal—*augury, divination, dowsing*—

that realm. The word *augury* is derived from the practice of interpreting omens from the observed flight of birds. When the observer, known as the *auger*, interprets these signs, it is referred to as *taking the auspices*. *Augur* and *auspices* are from the Latin *auspicum* and *auspex*, literally "one who looks at birds." In Rome, an auger would set a chicken loose amid corn scattered near letters set in a circle. Letters left untouched formed the basis of his predictions. Our word *auspicious* comes from it, as in, *Today is an auspicious day to begin*. I looked at the shape the spill made on the floor. It was a shape that kept forming, re-forming. At one point it looked like Florida—what could it possibly mean, what could one read into that?

When I was my daughter's age I remember standing on the edge of the saltmarsh down the road from my house. If I were there now I'd write the word REFUGE on a piece of cardboard and hold it up to the water. I'd want the marsh to know what it meant to me, when I was eight, how grateful I was (GRATITUDE) that she let me cross her every morning on my way to school. That she never pulled me under.

Even so, there were many ways to vanish into a marsh. A nail sticking out of a rusty board, the board once part of a ship, the ship broken apart in a storm one hundred, two hundred years ago. Or that storm window, the glass now daggers, blown out last winter by yet another storm. Or the mosquitoes, their tiny hypodermics filling your ears. Or the canals, dug in an attempt to control those same mosquitoes, each deep enough to swallow a child.

I lost a sneaker in one once.

I fell in trying to jump across one once.

I cut my palm once on a broken Coke bottle poking up through the muck.

Yet inside that marsh I never felt safer. No one could surprise me there, I'd always see them coming.

My GRATITUDE for that REFUGE was STUPID.

home

THIS MORNING, FLIPPING THROUGH A magazine, I find this comic: two rats in a sewer, one says to the other, *Do you ever wish that a different place felt like home?* I clipped it out, yet it took me all day to realize it mirrored a postcard that's been pinned over my desk for the past three years. In that postcard a man rises up from underground, in a city that looks like New York. He has pushed a grate in the sidewalk open, as if it were a door, his body now halfway risen from the earth. One hand holds the grate open, the other balances his body on the sidewalk. Now that I look at it again, he could be either rising up or sinking down, there really is no way to know, except by the look on his face, which I would call "furtive." Furtively he reenters the world of light, furtively he lowers himself into the darkness. Bearded, so it is hard to tell if that is soot on his face. His palms are both facing down, so it is hard to know if they need washing. His shirt is black, like that of everyone who spends time underground. *Do you ever wish that a different place felt like home?*

It seems obvious now that the rat comic and this postcard were stitched together by—in—my subconscious, though it wasn't obvious at the time: the rats are trapped in a filthy room with a grate for a ceiling; the grimy man is rising up from this same room.

I'd sometimes glimpse a rat in the marsh, rummaging around a canal, though this is not something I'd allow myself to think about much. This is what I once believed—that each rat contains an entire night, that when the sun goes away the world is revealed as being made primarily of rats. Yet I have never heard of rats being used for divination, maybe because it is so obvious: when you see a rat in any corner of your house something has already gone badly, deeply wrong. Life has already gone off the rails. *This*, the rat says, *is your future. I am your future.* My earliest memory is of being alone in a dark room, locked in the cage of my crib, the red eyes of a rat getting bigger, closer . . . Is this real, or simply a manifestation of some ancient terror?

Jung offers this: *The dread and resistance which every natural human being experiences when it comes to delving too deeply into himself is, at bottom, the fear of the journey to Hades.* Hades, I think, refers to the underground world we each carry within us, like that man rising up from the grate in the sidewalk, the grate you have to step over every day on your way to work. You never thought of it as a door. Yet you found it one day, it led underground, you didn't tell your wife where you'd go once she turned off the light. Down there it was always night. Maybe you imagined you'd like who you found down there, maybe you imagined it'd be like fucking someone with the lights out, how in the dark they could be anyone, as you'd reach out your hand, as if blind, to feel your way forward. I used to be on my way somewhere, now I am simply here. My daughter looks around our apartment, as if she'd just woken up on another planet. *Something is wrong.* I am her father, but some days (*surprise, surprise*) I have no idea what that means. When she was born I told myself, over and over, that she is the instruction manual, just pay attention. So I did, I paid attention, for years on end, then for a few years I drifted away, as if it was all just too much. This day. This life. Drifting, some days I was like the man rising up from the hole in the sidewalk, and some days I was like the man on a card from that tarot deck my friend made, the man who holds a spool of film in each hand. In that card, the mask I wear makes my head look like a skull, or maybe it is a skull. My daughter looks at this card. Why is there a snake around your neck? she asks. Is that why you're dead? The movie goes on and on, it is on an infinity loop. We sit in the dark and watch it, one spool spinning into the next. You can play the film in any direction—it can rewind, it can jump forward. In one scene my daughter's feet are blue, as blue as an eggplant. It was the winter of her birth. I thought her little blue feet were beautiful. I didn't know I needed to swaddle her. Someone came by our apartment, a friend who also happened to be a doctor, told me, *Put some clothes on that child.* In the next scene my daughter looks around this same apartment and says, *Something is wrong.* When did she learn to speak? Can I rewind the words back inside her? Here's what was, here's what will be, all of it held in this one spool of film.

snowglobe

A FRIEND WHO GREW UP in the same town as me (Scituate) sent me a photograph recently, something he saw in the news—our saltmarsh, completely submerged. The ocean is rising, swallowing the marsh, which has swallowed so much already. *If you become the aliment and the wet,* Whitman promised, *they will become flowers, fruits, tall branches and trees.* What, then, will our saltmarsh become? Back home, my mother warned me, every day it seemed, that (like the marsh) she would not be around forever. That I needed to get ready. Her words were a saltmarsh, filled with debris, each slowly being swallowed. It has taken me a lifetime to pick through each one.

Get ready.

Then she was dead.

Oh . . . that's what you meant.

A year later I found myself working at a homeless shelter, another refuge. Midway through that journey, my father showed up at the shelter door, homeless and needing a bed. Where once my mother had been home, my father had always been a ship—now one was on fire, and the other was sinking.

This morning I looked around—the white table, the enormous photograph of that ruined laundry—something was wrong. That photograph, by the way, is fake—it is a room you cannot enter, it's a tiny diorama created by the artist—I think of it as a handmade apocalypse, which is also the way I think of my poems, and (until recently) of my marriage. Or this: marriage is a car being driven down a dark highway at night. The interior overhead light makes the whole scene seem frozen, like a snowglobe. Someone is in the passenger seat, looking at a map. The driver, his or her hands tight on the wheel, is listening for the turn, or for the word *turn*. That's what marriage had seemed to be—a snowglobe with a little handmade apocalypse inside. A snowglobe waiting for someone to reach out a hand and shake it. This was when I believed that no one really wants to know what's to come, that we can barely bear what we've done to get here.

brook street

THE MOON LAST NIGHT ROSE big and red, so the tide today will be very high. If we try to walk it, the saltmarsh will be sloppy, impassable. It doesn't matter, that isn't the plan. This is our last road trip back to Scituate, we roll in around noon. My daughter is with me—where else would she be, if not with me?

First, as always, we stop at Maria's, to get our subs. Midday, so there's a line. Five Coast Guard guys come in behind us, each a version of the other—same body, same head, same blue suit. The girl making my sub spends some time picking something out of my roast beef over the trash. I don't want to know what it is. When we're done eating we step back out into the sunlight.

The rule, which is only in my head, is that we will only go to the places I'd go to when I was her age—the Harbor, the saltmarsh, Mr. Mann's. And, of course, to the house on Brook Street, across from the fire station, where we lived from the time I was five until I was eight. We'd done a slow drive-by on our last trip. It looked exactly like it did when I lived there.

This time, I simply go up to the door and knock. A guy answers. Hey, buddy, I say, though I don't remember saying this, nor do I know why I would call this stranger *buddy*, but my daughter insists I did. Hey, buddy, this is the house I grew up in. I was wondering if I could take a look around. His name is Peter. He says, Sure, why not? I have my book with me, I offer it to him. I'm this guy, I say. He says, Sure, I heard of you. Stephen Donovan told me you used to live here. Peter opens the door, we cross the threshold. I hadn't been inside for nearly fifty years. I expect it to be changed, mixed-up, like my dreams, but nothing is changed. It is as if it has been waiting for me to come back. Closer, some things are different, but everything is still in the same place. The kitchen is where the kitchen had been, but now there is a bathroom off the end of the dining room. The back shed, the one that had caught fire, is now open into the kitchen, like a mudroom. Peter tells me that when he got the place the back shed was a mess, falling down, nothing, really. He had to start from scratch. Peter had bought the place in 1989 (maybe he said 1999?), a long time ago—twenty or thirty years after we'd left. I don't know why we'd left, except to escape the fire. We were about to walk on the moon, Manson was about to record his first song. Peter was my age, he'd been in his late twenties or late thirties when he bought the place. The building inspector came in after he'd closed, condemned it. The floor in the kitchen was sinking—Peter kept reaching for the ceiling but it kept getting farther away. He tells us that he had five thousand dollars' worth of concrete poured in, that he made a slab and put the kitchen on it. He raised his family there, but now Peter's wife is gone. She left me with the house and the dog, he tells us. For now, he adds, suggesting she might come back for the dog. He has concert t-shirts draped on everything—KISS, Def Leppard. He'd found a pair of Advent speakers at a junk sale for five dollars—the neighbors didn't like it when he cranked them. He plays Cheap Trick for us—"I

Want You to Want Me"—my daughter and I put our fingers in our ears. The stereo is in the dining room, a whole wall of stereo, stereos everywhere. He likes his music, it's his *thing*. He reaches up to the ceiling again. When I tore off the back shed, he says, I found evidence of a fire. Up here, he says, running his hand along the lintel. It is still blackened. That's where the fire started, I say, in the back shed. And here is where my mother's bedroom was, I say, standing in the middle of a room that is no longer there. I don't know where she slept before the fire. On a blackboard in the kitchen someone has chalked, *IS IT TIME TO GIVE A FUCK?* which to me suggests that it isn't. We go into the living room. Peter tells us that he ran out of money at some point, or energy, or fucks to give, and so the living room was left untouched. By untouched I mean it is exactly the same as I had left it, fifty years earlier. The windows are the same, the front door, the staircase leading up. I can make out a tiny handprint on a windowpane—could it be mine? The staircase is steeper than I remembered. I don't mention tumbling down it through the smoke. It seemed we could have stayed there all day, it seemed we could have moved in, that Peter wouldn't have cared. He lived with his dog and his brother-in-law, his ex-wife's brother, whose room we couldn't enter—it was the one room we couldn't enter. Peter stood blocking our way. He's an animal, Peter said, or, The room's filthy, or something like that. It's the room we used to huddle in to watch *Laugh-In*, Monday nights on our tiny black-and-white tv. We're now upstairs. The bathroom is untouched as well. Here is the tub I was bathed in, here is the toilet I watched Vernon piss into, amazed at the number of bubbles his piss formed. A forceful stream.

Like a stone skipping across a pond, my daughter is now the age I was when our house caught fire. I kiss the top of her head, like my mother did. I breathe her into me, like smoke. I am holding the hand of my daughter in the house my mother set on fire when I was her age. I could briefly, at that moment, see it—my mother, in this room, holding my hand, flickering on when *she* was seven. This was when her father came home from his war, wearing his uniform of silence. Something happened to her when she was seven, you can see it in her school photographs. How, from one year to the next, her face changes, how a shadow creeps in. Something happened, some *annihilation*, and so when she held my hand she was forced to relive it, whatever it was, and she passed that something on to me. We're in the kitchen of the house on Brook Street, the first home my mother made for herself, after she left the home she was born into. But the only way for her to stay inside is to burn it all down.

Outside, beside the front door, the house now has a plaque on it, 1870-something, Moses-something. I don't know who put that up, Peter tells us. We're standing on the front steps, the steps I sat on with my mother, in that photograph taken by Vernon, before the fire, the one where she's holding me tight. I get Peter to take a picture of me and my daughter.

In the photo, I hold her the same way my mother held me.

plastic cathedral

CERTAIN PINECONES (FIRE CONES) WAIT centuries for a forest fire to release their seed. Without a fire nothing will grow. Certain stories can live inside us for years, hidden away, steering. To make something of this life, the idea of it, is sometimes a hard thing to face, day after day. Some mornings you wake up at the crack of doom, asking, What have I done with my days? You look in the mirror, yet where are you? What has this day, each day, made of you? What have you made of each hour? My daughter woke up this morning crying—she had overslept. School doesn't start for an hour, I gently point out. We can see the school out our front window, it's just down the block. Some mornings it's as if too much is crammed into too small a space. In this it mirrors what we now know about black holes (in this it mirrors this book). While I was writing this book the first photograph of a black hole was released worldwide. In order to capture it an international team of scientists had to coordinate a dozen telescopes, all over the world, to aim at a precise spot in the universe at a precise moment. They had to make a telescope the size of the earth.

Each Christmas, my grandmother would take a plastic cathedral out of a box stored in the attic, set it up on a side table in the living room, and plug it in. It was about the size of a mailbox. If you wound it up it would play "Silent Night" over and over. After a few minutes the song gradually slowed, the notes spaced further and further apart, as if it were being beamed into the far reaches of outer space.

A light bulb hidden inside made the entire thing glow.

I never saw my grandmother go into a real church, yet this one was given a sacred spot. Christmas, for my people, is simply a reason to get drunk and weepy. My grandmother's cathedral was molded out of creamy yellow plastic, sold by a company called Raylite. The doors wouldn't open, the round stained-glass window over the entry the same yellow as the roof. It would appear right after Thanksgiving, and remain until just after New Year's Day. For those few weeks its light never went out, creamy in the early dark. I'd stop by it on my way to the bathroom, put my face close, peer into the opaque windows. I'd wind it and the song would follow me down the hall.

The day after we see a photograph of a black hole for the first time, Notre Dame Cathedral burns. Workers had left dry lumber scattered on the roof like tinder. After the flames were put out, Jesus still hung over the altar. Some saw this as a sign, but a sign of what? Some even saw Jesus in the flames as it burned. The Christmas after our house caught fire my grandmother's plastic cathedral looked different. I'd watched my house, just a few months earlier, glowing from the inside. *Raylite cathedral becomes burning house becomes Notre Dame*—a bright red thread could connect them.

mister mann

MR. MANN LAY DOWN ONE NIGHT and in the morning he didn't get up. It began as sleep, like every other night, but it went on like that, this time forever.

After three years, my therapist asks me, What does Mr. Mann represent to you? Is he a body in a bed? Is he standing in a field with a shotgun? Or is he both? At this moment, I cannot tell if he is sleeping or frozen, aiming or waving.

Here's what I told my therapist:

Mr. Mann represented a place where I could control the damage. Before I found him I was forever wondering what might be coming next. When I was in his fields I knew, as long as I kept my eye on his door, that no one would ever be able to surprise me. I knew he had a shotgun, I just had to keep my eyes open. Then it hit me: Mr. Mann represented safety. He both knew I was there and he knew that I didn't want to be seen. In this way he was, in a way, kind. I was seven, I wasn't as clever as I'd like to imagine. I was spacey, a daydreamer. I talked to myself. In my pocket I kept a tiny stuffed monkey named Jocko—that was the name written on the tag around his neck. If Mr. Mann had wanted to unload a blast of rock salt on me it would have been easy to do so.

Before my therapist's question, I thought Mr. Mann was an unknowable god, like the Kabbalah talks about, but it turns out that was my mother. Imagine being twenty-seven—single, broke, two kids. Your boyfriend is married, he has kids of his own. What goes on in your bedroom is your business. But it is starting to seep out. Open *The Book of Creation*—here are your children, here is the home you have made. Open *The Book of Splendor*—it is all possibility. Your boyfriend will leave his family, you will be able to start again. Look into the flame—can't you see the face of splendor?

At the edge of a black hole, at its rim, is what is known as the event horizon—*a smoke ring framing a one-way portal to eternity*. In what way, though, is this any different from what we call death? It is only there, and only briefly, that we can see what is about to be lost.

The night Mr. Mann died I could have crawled in through a window to save him. I knew how to do that, I had that in me. I could have walked him around, made him keep talking. I knew from the movies that, when it's that cold, if you sleep you die. I knew in the end it wasn't so different— sleep, death.

This is what we would have spoken of:

> *Mann:* At some point it feels good, the cold.
> *Boy:* That's what I've heard.
> *Mann:* At first it's bad, but not for long.
> *Boy:* When you were little did you know it would end like this?
> *Mann:* I knew it might.

Boy: Were you afraid?

Mann: Not really. Earlier tonight it was as if I had entered a long hallway. I knew as soon as I opened the door.

Boy: I used to watch you, you know.

Mann: I know.

Boy: Every day, I'd pull myself through your field on my belly.

Mann: I saw. It got so I waited for you.

Boy: Why didn't you say anything? Why didn't you chase me away?

Mann: It didn't seem you had anywhere to be chased to.

Boy: I thought you had a shotgun.

Mann: I do have a shotgun.

Boy: Grandma said you shot a kid with rock salt.

Mann: I know. People said that.

Boy: Did you?

Mann: Not really. But it made things easier, that reputation.

Boy: I stole wood from your barn.

Mann: I let you steal it.

Boy: I broke into your house.

Mann: The door was unlocked.

Boy: I went in through the window. I stole a scroll.

Mann: I had lots of scrolls.

Boy: *Nicholas Nickelby.*

Mann: I didn't miss it.

Boy: What's the matter?

Mann: I'm just going to lie down for a minute.

Boy:　You have to stay awake. You have to keep
　　moving.

Mann: I left things for you to find. A can of rusty
　　nails, a broken hammer.

Boy:　That was you?

Mann: You were a good carpenter.

Boy:　I set your second field on fire once.

Mann: I saw.

Boy:　I should have been more careful.

Mann: I stood in the blackness and took a bit of ash
　　and spit into it and rolled it in my palm until I
　　could hear the grass crackle again.

Boy:　I didn't know you could do that.

Mann: You will learn.

Boy:　I wish you didn't have to go.

Mann: I was here a long time.

asteroid

ON THE THIRD ANNIVERSARY of my mother's death I took a bus to Mexico City. I was twenty-five. I got on in Juárez and twenty-four hours later got out in DF. That day of travel turned out to be Dia de Guadelupe, one of the biggest festivals in Mexico. Each town we rolled through was alive with parades, banners, fireworks. Hundreds of years ago the Virgin Mary had appeared to a man, to tell him where to build a church. She appeared to him five times. The last time, when he was doubting himself, she asked, *Am I not here, I who am your mother?* A couple weeks later, on Christmas Eve, I found myself in a church in Chiapas. It had been abandoned a couple years earlier, and now seemed more animist than Catholic—necklaces of fruit hung from the saints, the pews had all been removed. Worshippers sat in tight little circles, a candle in the center of each. Someone ran an egg over an infant's forehead, murmured a few words. *No estoy yo aquí, que soy tu madre?* From outside, the candles made the little church glow.

The villagers in Chiapas had shot a tourist for taking a photograph inside that church the year before I got there, so I didn't take any photos. This morning, on the radio, a man is reporting from Maracaibo, the second largest city in Venezuela. The power in the entire country has been out for two days. It is hot. The food, what little remains, is spoiling. In Maracaibo, after two nights without light, the people break into a supermarket. Inside, it is even darker than on the streets. Someone impales a roll of paper towels on a broom handle, sets it on fire, like a torch. A crowd fills the nearly empty aisles. More torches are lit. A mother takes bottles of baby formula. A boy grabs a sack of rice. Beans, cooking oil, salt, whatever can be carried away is carried away. The produce is rotting, the meat gives off a deathly smell, but this too is taken. They push the torches into boxes of cereal, the boxes catch fire, slowly at first, then they are ablaze. Like that, the whole aisle of cereal is lit up. Like that, the flames jump from aisle to aisle. The power came back on the next day, but nothing was left of the supermarket but ash. As if waking from a dream, no one could say exactly what had happened. They were hungry, they were desperate. On the radio someone says, *We lit the fires not to burn the building down, but simply to see what it was we were stealing.*

I can remember being twenty-seven, the age rock stars die. How stark it was, how my life was simultaneously spread out before me but also measurably over. Look at my mother one last time, as she fans the glowing coals out along our back deck. This is the first house she will buy, she won't take a dime from her father (not that a dime was offered). Her children are still asleep upstairs—from this night onward they will always be asleep upstairs. This is her event horizon, this is the last moment for her to see what she is losing. Look at the people of Maracaibo, in the hours and days after the power went out, how quickly the desperation set in.

When I first got sober, and for two years into it, I was on my own event horizon. I would say, if asked, that my truth was that I loved being sober, but that I also loved being fucked up. I was holding onto the edge of the rim, I was on the edge of losing myself forever. In the midst of the affair I was, again, holding on to the edge, ready to let go. I loved S, but I didn't understand how much I loved my wife. I didn't understand that love, like everything, is a daily practice. Yet some small glittering part of me wasn't ready to let go. I was offered a glimpse of what was about to be lost forever.

For now, the stories I tell my daughter need to be simple, elemental. There was a fire, an animal set it, we all were saved. I know it is incomprehensible. I tell her that afterwards I spent a lot of time in the woods behind my grandmother's. I built a treefort. I set a field on fire. I broke into a house. I stole a scroll. Do I tell her that I now believe that Mr. Mann wouldn't kill me, that I now believe he was looking out for me, that I didn't know where else to be? I tell her how my grandmother would pull a plastic cathedral out of a box each Christmas and plug it in. How the entire thing glowed. It's the same with the night our house was on fire—you cannot imagine how beautiful it was, to stand on the lawn and see each window lit up. And that supermarket in Maracaibo, think how it must have been, for those few moments, after smashing the glass, after rushing inside, when someone lit the first torch. How, after the hours and days of hunger building, how for a few moments the tops of each can glowed. Look into the flame—pure splendor. Not everything is ruins. Maybe my mother set our house on fire not merely to collect the insurance money, but simply to see what it was she was losing.

I tell my daughter the story of the last ice age, how one thing led to another. How when that asteroid hit the Yucatán, a column of fire rose up from the earth halfway to the moon. How minerals in the earth were liquefied, thrown into the atmosphere, only to harden and fall like rain. These glass raindrops—which we now call tektites—as they fell to earth, signaled the end of one era and the beginning of another. If not for that asteroid and the glass rain we'd be dinosaurs now, I tell her, instead of this.

Glass rain—I'd have liked to have been there for that.

It sounds unimaginably beautiful.

I'd like to hold a tektite in my hand.

My daughter offers to buy me a bowl of them.

She even finds some on the internet, for $2.49 each.

She knows now where I am from (which is where she is from), that town formed by a glacier receding. She's seen it, she's walked it. But the truth is I am from the bottom of the ocean, that is where my mother found me. She'd swum down to the bottom as a girl, she wasn't planning on coming back up, but there I was, a small glittering thing. She carried me up to the surface, placed me inside her girl body, and I grew. It was winter when I emerged—the ocean frozen over, the car wouldn't start, keys wouldn't turn in the locks. By the time of the fire it was the middle of August. My mother looked out at the ocean, counting the waves. Every seventh was big enough to carry us out, beyond sight. The town would go on, with or without us. The package store bell would bong when a customer entered, yet it would always be the same customer, it would always be my grandmother. The bank would lock its vault each night, yet someone would always find a way to break in. The record store would still play the latest hit, and sometimes it was a song we still listen to. *And I think it's going to be a long long time.* Jimmy and Buddy, the brothers who started Maria's, would still dice their tomatoes and pickles into cubes, like nowhere else in the universe. It was all comforting and suffocating, as if we'd never surfaced, as if we were still holding our breath, still searching for that one promised, glittery thing.

Yet here we are, it is all around us.

what we ate

YESTERDAY I WROTE THE WORDS *doctor appointment* in the log in the principal's office at my daughter's elementary school. I stood at the front desk, the log open in front of me. I considered writing the truth—*sometimes my daughter and I just get in the car and drive.* The log, though, made it clear that every other child from her classroom who'd skipped out of school early that month (there weren't many) had been pulled out because of a doctor appointment. I considered writing *restlessness*, but instead simply copied the entry before mine.

The truth is I was due to talk on a panel the next morning at a poetry festival. The topic of the panel was addiction. My wife was out of town, our child care had fallen through, so my daughter and I were taking the Megabus to Boston. My friend Tom had told me that the Breeders were playing that night, and he had access to a couple tickets. How could I deny my ten-year-old daughter this, her first grrrl power concert?

The bus ride was supposed to take four hours, but it ended up taking over five. We passed the time. We did a few exquisite corpses, we read a little, we looked out the window. We watched a disc of *Beasts of the Southern Wild*, which, as you may know, is narrated by a six-year old girl.

At first I'd pause the disc every few minutes to transcribe (imperfectly) a bit of evocative dialogue onto my phone:

> *The whole universe depends on everything fitting together just right . . . if one piece busts, even the smallest piece, the entire universe will get busted. . . .*

This idea of the universe breaking began to echo through the film:

> *The entire universe depends on everything fitting together just right . . . if you can fix the broken piece, everything can go right back . . .*

It echoed alongside the idea of everything being broken:

> *Sometimes you can break something so bad it can't go back together.*

A lot of things were breaking on the screen—plates were thrown, guns were shot, a trailer set on fire, a storm was coming, the ice shelf was melting, prehistoric beasts were set loose in the swamps. They looked a little like wild sheep. At one point my daughter took the phone from me and began taking notes herself:

> *When you small you got fix what you can.*

What she heard was different than what I heard. Her notes showed me something inside her that I hadn't yet glimpsed:

> *I gotta get strong.*

I yanked her out of school one day a couple years ago and we took the A train to Coney Island. She was seven years old then, she'd lived in Brooklyn her whole life, yet she'd never been to Coney Island. What kind of father was I? We rode on a few rides, put our feet in the ocean, gave some money to the carnies, ate a hot dog. She doesn't even remember that day, but I have to believe it is somewhere inside her, lurking in her cells.

On these trips I always bring a sack of food—Clif bars, veggie chips, chocolate, apples, clementines. As we watched the film we ate our way through it. The father in *Beasts of the Southern Wild* was both dying and a drunk. He always had a whole chicken waiting in a cooler, at dinnertime he'd stick it with a big fork and throw it onto a grill. He wasn't what you'd call a *good* father—verbally abusive, physically abusive—but he stuck around until he died. He was teaching his daughter how to survive.

Here are a few recipes from *Beasts of the Southern Wild:*
> a whole chicken from a cooler, forked onto a grill
> cat food mixed with canned gravy, sauteed in a big pot
> a crawfish/crab boil
> a catfish, caught by hand and punched in the head

The Megabus makes one stop, halfway through, at a gas station. We were told we had fifteen minutes to pee and get more food. It reminded me of that time in my life when gas stations were the only place I'd eat. At the time this phase seemed endless, though it only lasted about a year, maybe two. The year after my mother died, when every sunrise would find me asleep in my car. The year I always seemed to be driving, but I didn't get anywhere. I was a vegetarian when she died so I figured I should remain a vegetarian after she died. I was living on coffee, smoking a lot of pot, both of which I thought of as types of food.

Here's the recipe:

one pound of coffee
one bag of marijuana
a lighter (matches will do)

I was living in Massachusetts, not far from where I was born. I was rebuilding a boat, which was on land, trying to get it ready to go in the water. The plan was to live on it once—if—I got it floating. It would be my home. It was raised into the air on jacks. I was putting in twelve-hour days. Some nights I'd end up falling asleep on it, which was better than sleeping in my car. When I woke I'd make a pot of oatmeal. If I had raisins or nuts or maple syrup I'd add them, but I usually only had the oats, if that.

Here's the recipe:

one cup of oats
two cups of water
boil the water, add the oats.
let it simmer until a spoon can stand up in it
add whatever else is lying around

My daughter pauses the disc:

Everybody loses the thing that made them . . .
it's even how it's supposed to be in nature.

The days were getting short, the sun was going down. I had so much to learn. I wasn't much of a carpenter, and even if I were, a carpenter is not a boat-builder. Another day slipped inside itself. Now the sun was down, and I'd forgotten to eat, again. I could make more oatmeal but I knew I should get out. I hadn't spoken to a soul all day. The nearest place was a gas station, the nearest place is always a gas station. The lights were on, inside was well lit. I was a vegetarian, so I avoided the Slim Jims. I went to the chip aisle, got a big bag. I can't remember which brand, by then I didn't have a *brand*. Then I got a container of cottage cheese. I'd sit in my car in the parking lot, scraping the chips, one by one, into the cottage cheese, until both were gone.

Here's the recipe:

one large bag of potato chips
one container of cottage cheese

This was the fourth year in a row my daughter and I had made this road trip to Boston, but this was the first time we didn't go to Scituate. Maybe we were done with Scituate, maybe (for now) I'd shown my daughter all I could remember. We'd been to Mr. Mann's, we'd walked my saltmarsh, we'd stood inside the house on Brook Street. Peter had reached his hand up to the lintel to show us where the fire had started. Mr. Mann's falling-down house is now a museum. The house on Brook Street, even if forever unrenovated, had seen whole lives unfold within it since we'd left. Only the saltmarsh is the same, if now littered with some tasseled asshole's golf balls.

I began my first book, twenty years ago, with a quote from Winnicott:

It is joy to be hidden but a disaster not to be found.

That was when being hidden was the safest place to be. That was before I had become a father. Now I read Winnicott for his ideas about the "good-enough mother." This, these days, is my mantra, my goal—to be good-enough. I won't be here forever. This book in your hands—can this be called a "transitional object?"—even this, I see it as simply "good-enough." I am not my daughter, she is not me. Soon my daughter will be a teenager, soon she will enter the years when I went off the rails. It is possible I wandered in the infant's world of illusion and hallucination too long. Maybe I replaced the terror I felt in my home with a man in the woods who may or may not have had a shotgun. It was all stories swirling around me. The orphan grew up and wrote about the fire and the forest and he did it so he wouldn't have to feel any of it. It is possible that since my mother was always leaving, always telling me she was leaving, I was never able to see her as separate from my own self. It is possible, as my first girlfriend (O) said, I was weaned too early. I tell my daughter that I am not going anywhere, that I will always be here for her, even though this is, of course, another lie. One day I will die, and one day her mother will die, and she will be left to find her way. I hope—trust— she will find her way. I hope her way is not the tired path our people have wandered so long, of suicide, madness, addiction. I'm trying to teach her to be kind to all of the voices inside her, to be kind to all the beings she encounters. I will be here to answer any questions, as long as I can, to gently point out which path might actually lead out of the forest.

My daughter pauses the disc:

> When it all goes quiet behind my eyes I see everything that made me, flying around in invisible pieces.

When I look too hard, it goes away. But when it all goes quiet, I see they are right here. I see that I'm a little piece of a big, big universe, and that makes things right. When I die, the scientists of the future, they're gonna find it all.

gratitude

Love, if you are reading this now, please know I tried.

I made you an egg.

I gave you a knife.

Then a box of matches. Then I let you cook your own egg. Then I walked you across a saltmarsh. Then I showed you a car with a tree growing out of its roof. Then I told you a story of a hermit and his shotgun. I taught you about rock salt, nor'easters, and scrolls. You were too young, then you weren't. I wanted you to know where you came from, to wade up to your knees in saltwater. To never turn your back on a wave. I wanted you to know where your father came from. Love, it is possible that the practice of augury can help us let go of all that has been holding us in one place, to imagine it as something else. Augury takes the past and the future and the now and settles it all into the earth like so much debris. Child, believe this: a chicken can spell anything by what she leaves untouched—nothing can be hidden from her. The story we tell about our childhoods, even the story you are telling now, as you are in the midst of it, each word is so much debris in a saltmarsh, being slowly swallowed into what we will end up calling LIFE. The marsh responds to each word we hold up to it, we know this now, or at least we can choose to believe it. GRATITUDE. The marsh is happy. STUPID. The marsh is confused. Our words are a saltmarsh.

This is your childhood, which will soon be your girlhood. The future, love, is both unwritten and inevitable.

extracts

Perhaps home is not a place but simply an irrevocable condition.

—james baldwin, *giovanni's room*

There can be few mothers who, trapped with a fractious, wailing, ungrateful baby, have not wished it momentarily removed, and then become afraid of the dark powers the wish might attract.

—hilary mantel, *wicked parents*

What is to give light must endure burning.

—victor frankl, *man's search for meaning*

The world becomes alive only to the person who herself awakens to it . . . If we are insensitive to the world, the world ceases to exist for us. When Sleeping Beauty fell asleep, so did the world for her.

—bruno bettelheim, *the uses of enchantment*

Nothing human is abhorrent to me.

—terence, *heauton timorumenos*

Had the price of looking been blindness, I would have looked.

—ralph ellison, *invisible man*

some notes

book one

epigraph *(what we first learn . . .)*, gaston bachelard, *the psychoanalysis of fire.*

the story of a million years *(when you go into a room . . .)*, david huddle, *the story of a million years.*

wool *(a loss of belief . . .)*, dj waldie, *holy land.*

synecdoche *(whoever has no house . . .)*, rainer maria rilke, "autumn day."

medea *(whither can I fly . . .)*, euripedes, *medea*; *(the truth must dazzle gradually . . .)* emily dickinson.

canopic *(fire is the ultra-living element . . .)*, gaston bachelard, *the psychoanalysis of fire; (we all have to learn to freeze . . .)*, joan didion, *the white album; (everything that lives is holy)*, william blake, *vala.*

happy jar *(some days, when I catch . . .)*, eduardo corral, *unpublished fragment.*

question (*you can run . . .*), nick flynn, "cartoon physics, part 1."

smoke (*trauma by its nature . . .*), bessell van der kolk, *the body keeps the score; (through fire everything changes . . .),* gaston bachelard, *the psychoanalysis of fire.*

this god (*somehow, when you consciously . . .*), fred alan wolf, *towards a quantum field theory of mind;* nina simone, *what happened, miss simone?* (*film*).

you can't always get what you want (*if we try to take apart something . . .*), michael talbot, *the holographic universe.*

book two

epigraph (*ladybug, ladybug . . .*), *traditional.*

six baby mice (*you're not from these parts . . .*), beckett, *waiting for godot.*

whirlpool (*the universe we experience . . .*), howard wiseman and michael hall, "quantum phenomena modeled by interactions between many classical worlds."

dead man's float (*the real death . . .*), henry miller, in a letter to anaïs nin.

polaroid kenneth josephson, *matthew, 1965.*

book three

epigraph (*each one wraps himself . . .*), dante, *inferno.*

dark energy robert duncan, "often I am permitted to return to a meadow."

listenerland mark epstein, *the trauma of everyday life.*

amber paranormal images culled from *into the unknown*, reader's digest books.

whose dream is this? (*the beautiful uncut hair . . .*), walt whitman.

bright thread (*drowning in flame*), charles bukowski.

the book of splendor (*I'm really looking forward . . .*), *the martian* (film); (*a stone is a thing . . .*), carlo rovelli, in conversation with krista tippett, *on being;* (*days pass and the years vanish . . .*), talmud.

find me when you wake up laurie anderson, in conversation with amanda stern, *the believer;* parker palmer, in conversation with krista tippett, *on being.*

centralia (*babies who are not adequately held . . .*), d. w. winn-icott, *collected writings.*

erasure (*out, damned spot*), shakespeare, *macbeth.*

doctor mee (*creepy always to want . . .*), via dan chiasson, *the new yorker.*

songline (*the shock of trauma . . .*), mark epstein, *the trauma of everyday life.*

beatrice (*the buddha did not always . . .*), mark epstein, *the trauma of everyday life; (after the new fear . . .),* rainer maria rilke, *florence diaries.*

annihilation (*we cannot literally go back . . .*), louis newman, in conversation with krista tippett, *on being;* ocean vuong, "someday I'll love ocean vuong."

jar of water (*everyday life is a trauma . . .*), mark epstein, *the trauma of everyday life.*

augury lori nix, *laundromat, 2008;* masaru emoto, *hidden messages in water.*

home rat cartoon (*do you ever wish . . .*), will mcphail, *the new yorker; (image of man rising from grate),* eugene richards, *new york city, 1988; (the dread and resistance . . .),* c. g. jung, *psychology and alchemy (tarot deck),* kahn / selesnick, *the carnival at the end of the world; (put some clothes on that child . . .),* dr. juliette widoff, private conversation.

mister mann (*a smoke ring framing . . .*), dennis overbye, "darkness visible, finally: astronomers capture first ever image of black hole," *the new york times,* 2019.

debts

gratitude *goes out to the organizations that provided essential time and support: the fine arts work center (provincetown); the atlantic center for the arts (new smyrna beach); the lannan residency fellowship (marfa); the university of houston; the djerassi resident artists program (woodside); the omega center (rhinebeck); the brooklyn writers space . . .*
gratitude *also goes out to friends who directed me toward useful sources: nuar alsadir, lou chamberlain, john chessia, susanna crossman, cindy cruz, carolyn forche, suzanne gardnier, clarisse gorokhoff, marie howe, j. kastely, marie-elizabeth mali, jamaal may, meghan o'rourke, dina peone, mark slouka, jacqueline woodson . . .* **gratitude** *as well to the students I've been blessed to work with over the years, especially those in workshops where many of these pieces were first manifest . . .* **gratitude** *always to the friends who kept me on track (or at least tried to) during the years of finding my way to this book (the sibling to this book—I will destroy you—has the full list) . . .* **gratitude** *to jill bialosky and all the brilliant and kind folks at norton . . .* **gratitude** *to bill clegg . . .* **gratitude** *to tad flynn . . .* **gratitude** *eternal to lili taylor and maeve flynn.*

acknowledgments

Ocean Vuong, excerpt from "Someday I'll Love Ocean Vuong" from *Night Sky with Exit Wounds*. Copyright © 2016 by Ocean Vuong. Reprinted with the permission of The Permissions Company, LLC on behalf of Copper Canyon Press, www .coppercanyonpress.org.

Excerpt from "Often I Am Permitted to Return to a Meadow" by Robert Duncan, from *The Opening of the Field*, copyright ©1960 by Robert Duncan. Reprinted by permission of New Directions Publishing Corp.

"Bag of Mice" and "Cartoon Physics, part 1 (excerpt)" from *Some Ether.* Copyright © 2000 by Nick Flynn. Reprinted with the permission of The Permissions Company, LLC, on behalf of Graywolf Press, graywolfpress.org.

"What You Can't Hear" from *I Will Destroy You*. Copyright © 2019 by Nick Flynn. Reprinted with the permission of The Permissions Company, LLC, on behalf of Graywolf Press, graywolfpress.org.

"As We Drive Slowly Past the Burning House" from *The Ticking Is the Bomb*, W. W. Norton. Copyright © 2010 by Nick Flynn.

"Synecdoche" (written for Jack Pierson) first appeared in *Provincetown Arts*, 2019. Chris Busa, ed.

"Canopic" first appeared in *Salmagundi*, 2017. Robert Boyers / Peg Boyers, eds.

"What You Can't Hear" first appeared in *The Bennington Review*, 2019. Michael Dumanis, ed.

"Wool" first appeared in *Knitting Pearls: Writers Writing about Knitting*, 2016. Ann Hood, ed.

"Whose Dream Is This?" first appeared in the catalogue *Jim Peters: A Retrospective*, 2013. PAAM.

"Sleeping Beauty," first appeared in *Guernica*, 2016; it was then included in the anthology *The Kiss: Intimacies From Writers*, W. W. Norton, 2018. Brian Turner, ed.

"What I Ate," first appeared in *Eat Joy: Stories & Comfort Food from 31 Celebrated Writers*, Black Balloon Publishing, 2019. Natalie Eve Garrett, ed.